Internet of Things

What You Need to Know About IoT, Big Data, Predictive Analytics, Artificial Intelligence, Machine Learning, Cybersecurity, Business Intelligence, Augmented Reality and Our Future

© **Copyright 2019**

All Rights Reserved. No part of this book may be reproduced in any form without permission in writing from the author. Reviewers may quote brief passages in reviews.

Disclaimer: No part of this publication may be reproduced or transmitted in any form or by any means, mechanical or electronic, including photocopying or recording, or by any information storage and retrieval system, or transmitted by email without permission in writing from the publisher.

While all attempts have been made to verify the information provided in this publication, neither the author nor the publisher assumes any responsibility for errors, omissions or contrary interpretations of the subject matter herein.

This book is for entertainment purposes only. The views expressed are those of the author alone, and should not be taken as expert instruction or commands. The reader is responsible for his or her own actions.

Adherence to all applicable laws and regulations, including international, federal, state and local laws governing professional licensing, business practices, advertising and all other aspects of doing business in the US, Canada, UK or any other jurisdiction is the sole responsibility of the purchaser or reader.

Neither the author nor the publisher assumes any responsibility or liability whatsoever on the behalf of the purchaser or reader of these materials. Any perceived slight of any individual or organization is purely unintentional.

Contents

INTRODUCTION 1
CHAPTER 1 – ORIGINS OF IOT 3
CHAPTER 2 – IOT SECURITY 7
CHAPTER 3 – ETHICAL HACKING 13
CHAPTER 4 – INTERNET OF THINGS 21
CHAPTER 5 – UNDER THE CUSHY FOOT OF TECH GIANTS 33
CHAPTER 6 – THE POWER OF INFINITE FUNDS 37
CHAPTER 7 – IOT TOYS 40
CHAPTER 8 – BIO-ROBOTICS 45
CHAPTER 9 – PREDICTIVE ANALYTICS 51
CHAPTER 10 – MACHINE LEARNING 58
CHAPTER 11 – ARTIFICIAL INTELLIGENCE 62
CHAPTER 12 – CYBERSECURITY 70
CHAPTER 13 – BIG DATA 78
CHAPTER 14 – BUSINESS INTELLIGENCE 83

CHAPTER 15 – AUGMENTED REALITY	88
CHAPTER 16 – VIRTUAL REALITY	94
CHAPTER 17 – OUR FUTURE	101
CONCLUSION	105
GLOSSARY	107

Introduction

You were just woken up in the middle of the night by smart lightbulbs in your house blasting at full power for no reason. Your bleary-eyed investigation shows they tried to download a firmware update and failed. At that moment, Alexa starts quietly whispering sweet nonsense to herself in the corner and Roomba starts slamming into the nearest wall. What do you do? Is your house haunted or have the machines finally started an uprising? Neither – it's just another day in the IoT wonderland.

The following book reveals the concepts and methods powering perhaps the most ambitious technological concept of the twenty-first century – the Internet of Things (IoT) – and parades all the ridiculously named gadgets techies imagined to saturate the market before the competition. Mystical, cheap and scalable, the idea of IoT attracts creative grifters of all shapes and sizes to try their luck in pushing yet another completely unnecessary gadget to the market in hopes of fleecing gullible buyers. What you're about to read contains all the juiciest examples of IoT technology, including:

- Smart sprinklers that can be turned on and off from halfway across the world
- A smart toilet with ambient lighting and speakers for total immersion
- Smart scented candles with the scent of money set on fire
- A smart fishing rod for gathering stats on the spot
- A smart air purifier that moves around the house
- A smart water faucet with LED lighting
- A smart menstrual cup
- A smart block of wood
- Smart bumblebees
- A smart padlock
- Smart farms

IoT shows amazing potential in medicine, where it can relieve doctors and nurses of daily drudgery related to managing chronic diseases, such as diabetes. In the meantime, satire and wishful thinking abound in IoT, presenting us with a glorious reality full of humor and head-scratching. *What were they thinking*? Well, let's find out.

Chapter 1 – Origins of IoT

You know that old song with the lyrics, "Foot bone connected to the heel bone; Heel bone connected to the ankle bone" and so on? If you imagine a vast, digital body spanning the entire world whose parts are connected just the same way as described in the song, except they're made of information and tiny gadgets, you'll come very close to the idea of IoT. Packets of data traveling back and forth in the global IoT body would then represent the nervous activity in a living body, where cells communicate with one another to coordinate and fulfill some greater purpose for the benefit of the entire organism. The definition of **IoT** would thus go: a series of devices with some ulterior purpose that has been given internet connectivity.

It's hard to say who, if anyone, conceived the notion of IoT but we can guess busy scientists looking to shave a fraction of a second off their interactions with the real world were the first to embrace the idea of interconnected gadgets and bring it to fruition. Because they didn't care about flashiness, their gadgets were crude and their protocols efficient, which minimized **attack surface**, joint weakness of a network that directly correlates with complexity. There is a way to deploy IoT in the real world securely, but it has to be done by professionals who know the risks and benefits.

During the 1970s, scholars of the Massachusetts Institute of Technology (MIT) were enjoying cold fizzy drinks from the campus' Coca-Cola vending machine at a discount price. The problem was that, as the campus grew, the drinks would be snatched up almost immediately by passersby at the expense of those on the outskirts of the campus, who had to walk ten or fifteen minutes just to find there's nothing in the vending machine, or worse yet, that it's just been refilled, and the sodas are still warm. So, there was an actual problem in a tightly-knit community that led to frustration and loss of productivity. As we're about to see, IoT *can help* in situations like these.

The vending machine received micro-switches in each of the six columns to keep tabs on when each bottle was placed inside and whether it was sufficiently chilled; after three hours, the central processor would mark the bottle as "cold" in the companion program. The vending machine was given its own user account in the internal campus network, allowing anyone to ping for user "coke" to check out the bottle status. Anyone hooked up to the internet who could access the campus network was capable of checking on whether bottles were chilled, though there wasn't much use in the function if you were halfway across the globe[1].

Note the organic process of how IoT became integrated with existing technology – members of a tightly-knit community were experiencing discomfort and loss of productivity due to outdated technology that provided insufficient information. By integrating small and highly specific IoT capability in the existing technology infrastructure, discomfort was averted, and productivity losses were minimized. There are plenty of ways to sabotage this particular IoT implementation, but any such saboteur would need physical access

---

[1] https://www.cs.cmu.edu/~coke/history_long.txt

to the campus, in which case he or she will be easily caught or identified. This is *not* how IoT will work for the general public. Instead of having specific features requested by customers, IoT devices will have a plethora of gimmicks that will open workplaces and homes across the world to relentless hacking attacks.

No single entity decided to create IoT; it's actually a spontaneously emerging network of loosely allied devices. Software and hardware industries are *aching* for a set of standards, and IoT seems to be the closest we'll get to a global interconnectedness standard. So, shower curtains from China, wool socks from Italy and coffee mugs from Argentina can all be given internet connectivity to turn them into IoT devices that can communicate, but the question is – why?

IoT actually allows companies to offset a part of their production cost by gathering and selling data of customers, hiding inflation in the process. The intrusion of privacy is still there, but it's much easier to ignore it when you appear to have saved 20% on the price of a shower curtain or a coffee mug. Sure, you'll be presented with a privacy policy or terms of use where the fine print states your use of the product will be tracked, but who reads those? When was the last time you read a 'terms of service', let alone the fine print in one? When a company sees that customers don't care about their privacy and starts blatantly spying through IoT functionality, then all companies have to start doing it or risk falling by the wayside.

On the practical side of things, IoT shower curtains can measure humidity in the bathroom and automatically open IoT windows to let some water vapor out when you're done showering. You did buy IoT windows, didn't you? IoT wool socks can measure circulation in your feet and alert when you should stretch or go for a walk, and an IoT coffee mug can display the time on its surface or just communicate with your IoT coffee table to warn you through an app that your coffee is getting cold. You did buy an IoT coffee table, right?

See how it works? Each IoT product provides a crumb of utility that only comes true when you buy the missing ten items that confer additional functions to the entire set. Oh, and buying another ten items unlocks this capability and another 100 items that one and so on. By acting upon the hoarding instinct inherent in all humans, companies producing IoT gadgets aim to make a fortune by peppering our living spaces with seemingly useful gadgets that do have a marginal advantage over non-IoT items in the same category but are otherwise just the same, except pricier and completely insecure.

Chapter 2 – IoT Security

In any network, the main principle regarding security is that the entire network is only as secure as its weakest link. How much security do you think an IoT shower curtain would have? Precisely zero because the manufacturer, most likely a Shenzhen factory, will be looking to minimize production costs and offset any liabilities onto the next link in the chain, such as IoT windows. Well then, how much security would IoT windows have? None whatsoever because the manufacturer of those would again be following the same logic of making the biggest profits.

Once a hacker hijacks any IoT device in a household, he or she will gain possession of them all in a cascading manner, turning the entire IoT network against the owner. Foot bone connected to the heel bone; Heel bone connected to the ankle bone… In one instance, a casino got its entire network compromised thanks to an IoT thermometer in a fish tank in the lobby[2]. The entire database of players was hacked into, copied and pulled out through that same thermometer and nobody was the wiser. It can take years before anyone notices these breaches of security, and even then, people in charge are likely just to shrug it off.

There is simply no set of IoT safety standards like there is with food, cars or bikes; anyone can make IoT devices and market them globally without any liability. There is no insurance against hacking attacks either, making the entire IoT field a haphazard endeavor, which is great for entrepreneurs that have nothing to lose but pretty rotten for regular people and businesses who are hyped for technology that end up getting burned. That doesn't mean IoT is useless, but simply that it has to be deployed in an environment that is already secure and with well-known, trusted users, just like we saw with MIT scholars and their soda machine. What happens when IoT is deployed insecurely worldwide? Hacking attacks, the scale of which dwarfs everything we've seen so far.

In 2016, a massive wave of internet signals smashed at the shores of US consumer devices and caused huge congestion in traffic. It came from IoT devices carelessly left online for anyone to hack into and take over. CloudFlare, the intermediary company that analyzes internet traffic and mitigates cyberattacks, studied this particular bout of distributed-denial-of-service attacks and found they were mostly coming from Vietnam and Ukraine[3] but were otherwise carefully orchestrated across thousands of different IP addresses. At times, the volume of traffic went over 1 million requests per second and consisted of 52,467 unique IP addresses. Analysis of attacker traffic showed that Vietnamese devices were most likely CCTV cameras due to ports they had opened.

---

[2]https://thehackernews.com/2018/04/iot-hacking-thermometer.html

[3]https://blog.cloudflare.com/say-cheese-a-snapshot-of-the-massive-ddos-attacks-coming-from-iot-cameras/

IBM's Chief Technology Officer (CTO), Bruce Schneier, warned in 2017 that governments have to take IoT security seriously and step up their game before the damage is done. He said, "We're building a robot the size of the world, and most people don't even realize it" in a keynote address at the SecTor security conference in November 2017[4]. What used to be cybersecurity now has to rapidly evolve to become "everything-security", implying there's no stopping the building of IoT, but we can at least minimize the vulnerabilities.

In January 2019, the Japanese government announced an IoT security project[5] during which sanctioned hackers will be scanning IoT networks and trying to breach routers and webcams on vulnerable networks in preparation for the 2020 Olympic Games. Hackers will be using what's known as a **dictionary attack**, meaning they will have a compiled list of all the most commonly used username/password combinations, such as "admin/admin" or "admin/blank". The list will presumably be forwarded to Japanese ISPs who will then alert the owners of those devices to change usernames and passwords. See any weakness in this plan? If a black hat hacker were to get a peek at that list, it would make their work a whole lot easier.

Why such fear? In 2014, the Winter Olympic Games held in Sochi, Russia, were protected by the heavily entrenched Russian army with over 40,000 law enforcement officers. Security checkpoints were set all over the place with X-rays and metal detectors while aerial patrols circled the skies and gunboats patrolled the sea. What about cybersecurity? Internet traffic was thoroughly analyzed, but Sochi was still besieged by hackers that set up plenty of traps for naive tourists who just wanted to get drunk and roll in the snow. For example, after arriving at the airport, a tourist gets a notification that

---

[4]http://www.eweek.com/security/ibm-s-schneier-it-s-time-to-regulate-iot-to-improve-cyber-security

[5]https://www.zdnet.com/article/japanese-government-plans-to-hack-into-citizens-iot-devices/

there's free Wi-Fi access as long as he or she downloads and installs a special app.

The trick is that the app is actually malware and captures passwords and banking information. Even when the tourist goes back home, he or she will often keep the app, which will continue to leech private information. Even if someone were to notice something fishy and figure out the app did it, can you imagine calling the police because of a malicious app? You'd probably get arrested and fined for being a nuisance. In this way, hackers use a low-risk, high-reward strategy that exploits laziness of a general smartphone user.

Anyway, that Russian athletes were doped up during Sochi Olympics came out later that year, with the governing body banning all Russian-affiliated athletes from the 2018 Olympics, which is when someone, supposedly Russian state-sponsored hackers, tried to hack the South Korean Olympic games. Dubbed "Olympic Destroyer"[6], this particular strain of malware was well prepared by someone who had inside knowledge of systems in place. Olympic Destroyer would nestle on an infected machine, steal passwords in an attempt to infect the entire network and then deliver coup de grace by completely wiping out everything from the machine, including any trace of infection. This led to some disruption to the opening ceremony and the Wi-Fi network in use, but otherwise, everything was smooth sailing.

Cybersecurity researchers later claimed that Russian hackers made Olympic Destroyer, but then another group of researchers said it was Chinese hackers. Well, which was it? Nobody can tell. All hacking attacks leave behind traces of information, but it's impossible to know if the hackers were simply sloppy or played mind games with researchers. That's the scariest part of IoT – the fact you could be sitting in your cozy Wyoming home playing "Fortnite" while Danish and Estonian hackers try to disrupt each other through your network,

---

[6]https://motherboard.vice.com/en_us/article/d3w7jz/olympic-destroyer-opening-ceremony-hack

using your devices and spending your power to mine cryptocurrencies or make DDoS attacks. Unless you have the cybersecurity expertise that can at least match hackers, you'd be none the wiser, and you'd be footing the bill. At least California is doing something to stop an IoT disaster.

In September 2018, California governor Jerry Brown signed SB 327[7], a cybersecurity bill meant to tighten up IoT security, slated to go into effect January 2020. Current cybersecurity law requires that a California business undertake "reasonable security procedures" to maintain the privacy and security of its customers; SB 327 aims to expand that to "reasonable security feature or features that are appropriate to the nature and function of the device". Whoop-de-do. Why are legislators so afraid of locking down digital technologies? The answer to that lies in China.

The Chinese government has quite an interesting mentality – economic victory at any cost. To match that the US government simply has to abrogate the constitutional rights of its citizenry, at least when it comes to making free market choices. By giving domestic companies plenty of legal and economic leeway, the US government foisted them as de facto arbiters of right and wrong in the country. This is why the 2008 credit crash in the US resulted in taxpayers bailing out banks that went all in and lost horribly; without a bailout, the Chinese would have swooped in, bought them off and then it would have been game over. So, anything China does, the US has to do to an extent or risk falling behind.

When applied to IoT, what this means is that regular citizenry will have their privacy invaded the same way Facebook and other such companies already do in order to generate value and stay competitive in the global economy. Sure, there will still be laws like SB 327, but they'll intentionally have loopholes so US companies can compete and be applied only when the general public gets so irate that it

---

[7]https://leginfo.legislature.ca.gov/faces/billTextClient.xhtml?bill_id=201720180SB327

needs a scapegoat. If you want some peace and privacy, you'll have to hack your way to it.

Chapter 3 – Ethical Hacking

In the context of IoT, ethical means "distinguishing between good and evil" and hacking means "unorthodox use of a system or tool for a palpable advantage." Without going into philosophy, good and evil refer to having a goal; good is whatever brings you closer to that goal and evil whatever makes you stray away from it. So, if your goal is to have privacy, then ethical hacking helps you achieve privacy through unorthodox use of systems or tools. Sound good?

One example of ethical hacking is overclocking graphics cards. In essence, manufacturers of graphics cards for desktop computers typically cap their strength anywhere between 80-95% of their full potential. By tinkering with graphics cards, it's possible to remove the cap on the internal clock they're using (hence *over*clocking) and unlock the performance that's already there but hidden away from the user. Thus, ethical hacking gets you what you paid for, but the company doesn't want to provide for whatever silly reason.

Keep in mind that the US government considers hacking a big no-no, but the legislators are mainly older people out of touch with technology who consider the internet "a series of tubes". As long as the ethical hacking you do isn't a nuisance and doesn't do harm or economic damage, you're pretty much under their radar. This applies to law enforcement as well, which is typically so overwhelmed with traditional crime that it has no time to deal with eccentrics tinkering with toys in their garage; again, unless you're being a nuisance or doing harm or damage. Don't attract any undue attention to yourself and keep working on your IoT customizations, which is all ethical hacking is.

Conversely, all hackers prosecuted in the US to date have had the charge of wire fraud levied against them. The definition of wire fraud is so mind-bogglingly broad that it includes intentional misrepresentation of fact to achieve deception through electronic means of communication. Essentially, girls posting their selfies with camera filters and puppy ears are committing wire fraud because they're misrepresenting their faces to deceive observers into thinking they're cuter than they are. Thus, if law enforcement wants to make an example out of you, they can find so many ways to do it.

Companies churning out IoT products are in a similar bind – they have deadlines to meet, half-baked products to push out and lawsuits to fend off. Everything they do is highly optimized to deliver maximum revenue. They have no time or resources to deal with each ethical hacker unless he or she is, you guessed it, being a nuisance or doing harm or economic damage. This leaves you plenty of space to actually get some of those God-given constitutional rights without interfering with companies on their revenue-gathering rampage.

The exact specifics of ethical hacking are a bit trickier. IoT technology advances so quickly that it's truly a thankless task to write any kind of tutorial on it, especially one that's meant to stand the test of time. However, technology is typically improved incrementally, meaning some underlying principles are likely to apply to several generations of IoT devices.

Ethical hacking is about taking things apart and watching them tick. So, when you get your hands on an IoT device that you won't feel sorry to see die, take it apart in controlled circumstances and watch how it ticks. This will show you how companies assemble their products and also underline how shoddily they're built – what with third world factories hastily assembling them for pennies. So, if you can take your time to understand any given IoT device and improve upon it, you've become an ethical hacker. Preferably, also disconnect it from the internet and don't let it contact its home server with a status report, which is what all IoT devices typically do. Also, keep in mind that about 95% of all domestic fires are started due to faulty electrical wiring.

IoT is also meant to be about short-range Wi-Fi and radio connections. Connectivity and low price take precedence over things such as privacy and reliability, so keep in mind that IoT is not meant to be safe. IoT is actually so thoroughly insecure that you should seriously investigate how Wi-Fi and RFID work and see if you can find ways to implement custom security protocols in your household before using a single IoT device. Exercise caution when experimenting with Wi-Fi and radio waves as doing that can get you in a whole other heap of trouble.

We know from news reports that these matters are investigated by the Federal Communications Commission (FCC), who takes its job seriously. In short, FCC is like the FBI with tuning forks that hunt down everyone who might think about messing with radio waves. In October 2017, a certain Jay Peralta[8] was fined $400,000 for interfering with NYPD radio systems by issuing a total of nine unlawful messages over police frequencies during 2016. Jay was charged with a total of 21 counts that included terrorist threats, aggravated harassment and filing false reports, carrying a twenty-year prison sentence.

---

[8] http://wirelessestimator.com/articles/2017/robber-who-threatened-to-kill-nypd-captain-gets-first-taste-of-justice-with-404k-fcc-fine/

Diagnostic tools are central to becoming an ethical hacker. Being able to estimate what's happening is one skill that might serve you up to a point, but knowing what's going on gives you tremendous power because correct information is the secret to living the fullest life imaginable. Which tools to choose and how are, again, ridiculously vague questions, but you can start with baby steps and slowly build your collection based on what you discover over the course of a few years.

Laziness is a key component in the complacency of the average US consumer. IoT companies are counting on consumers being too bored or too busy to pay attention to fine print or specifics. So, stay alert and pay attention to what's happening. Always try to get your hands on raw data and interpret it yourself rather than having a laugh-track pundit do it for you. If you can keep learning and improving your ethical hacking skill, you'll be outpacing these tech companies by leaps and bounds, allowing you always to stay ten steps ahead of them.

One vigilante hacker took it upon himself to test out IoT the best way possible – by **bricking** them, which means he destroys their functionality. The hacker's nickname is Janitor, and his malware is called BrickBot, with the sole purpose of scanning the internet for insecure IoT devices with default usernames and passwords to infect and corrupt their firmware[9], the essential code baked into the device. TVs, cameras, lightbulbs, toilets and everything else is all liable to be hit by BrickBot, and they'll all be made into expensive paperweights.

According to Janitor, 90% of all IoT cameras made by a certain manufacturer were set up with default passwords, allowing anyone to hack into them. What Janitor is doing is sadly a crime because there's still no legal consequence for having an insecure IoT device, but there is for downright destruction of property. So, what happens

---

[9]https://gizmodo.com/this-hacker-is-my-new-hero-1794630960

when IoT manufacturers start making medical implants or wearables with similar shoddy security and people start dying because of such lack of care?

What would happen if IoT devices were legally mandated to come with security warnings, such as "this device may cause a network to be hacked"? In California, every product sold already contains a warning label[10], but the obtusely vague Proposition 65 didn't mandate companies to tell consumers what exactly is dangerous, where it's found on or in the product, why it's there for or what the actual risks are. Without any of that information, how is the warning label meant to be of any use?

With buildings having to display these same warnings too, citizens started bounty hunting and suing those companies who didn't have enough warning stickers, so companies and individuals plastered them everywhere. Nobody can tell how many warning stickers are enough to make the company shielded under the law. So, with every product and area getting a "something in here may lead to congenital disabilities/cancer", customers simply blank them out of their consciousness and do their business anyway because we have to keep living no matter what.

This oversaturation with warning to the point of indifference is a problem observed with internet users, called banner blindness and is easily explained as attention withdrawal. We all have a limited amount of attention at our disposal. When something is boring to us, it means we've determined it unworthy of our attention and want to do something else. With banner blindness, the warning or information displayed shows itself as thoroughly useless to the point people actively block out anything looking like a banner. If you're surfing the internet from an EU location, you're probably already doing this whenever you dismiss the cookie warning banner – there's no useful information in the warning banner, so you simply ignore it.

---

[10]https://www.accountablescience.com/californias-warning-label-overload/

One humorous suggestion for warning labels presents "scientifically responsible"[11] warnings, such as "this product consists of 99.9999999999% empty space" and "some quantum physics theories suggest that when the consumer is not directly observing this product, it may cease to exist or will exist only in a vague and undetermined state." While scientifically correct, these warnings would likely freak out people curious enough to read them but not curious enough to research them. This is at the core of all the warning label drama – we can't make consumers care about what they're using until it's too late.

What we can do is educate ourselves as best as we can and try to do just a little bit of good for the world. Perhaps this can take the form of tutoring individuals on the dangers of IoT, writing blog posts or just talking to those in the vicinity on the topic when the opportunity arises. The mainstream media will never consider talking about IoT unless there's some outrageous context for it – a.k.a., if it bleeds, it leads. At least kids should be encouraged to tinker with IoT and improve it whenever possible, which would teach them ethical hacking from early childhood and also give them practical, engineering skills.

Though plenty of anarchist-oriented people involved with IoT scoff at the prospect of government regulation, the thing is that market incentives with IoT are chaotic, and there's no clear way for market forces to balance each other out within the current copyright and patent framework. Why should the producer of a cheap and widespread IoT device care if it's involved in a DDoS attack? Should the consumer care? What happens with a company's liabilities once it gets dissolved? What's to stop any given person from making a company, producing millions of IoT devices, reaping profits, shuttering the business and disappearing when customers start clamoring for security updates?

---

[11]https://stuff.mit.edu/people/dpolicar/writing/netsam/warning_labels.html

What governments can do is set soft limits on copyrights and patents in cases where the manufacturer of a device stops updating or maintaining it, perhaps even mandating that source code be made freely available in case the company is dissolved. In this way, the general public would be legally protected if it tried reverse-engineering devices and openly offering solutions to the IoT cybersecurity problem. Right now, there's no political will to think ahead; democratic elections lead to a constant rotation of elected officials, who have no incentive to offer long-term solutions, the results of which their political opponents can claim as their own. It's stupid, silly and egocentric but that's how it works and unless we upgrade our political process and our mindset, we'll be buried under a mountain of insecure IoT devices that are pretty much nobody's fault.

In one case, an IoT garage door opener manufacturer actually took revenge on an unhappy customer[12]. On April 1, 2017, a certain Martin left a vitriolic comment on the community forum related to Garadget, cursing the iPhone app. His comment got no replies. Soon after, Garadget's Amazon page got a negative review from Martin, which prompted Garadget's developer to block his device from the cloud services it needed to operate. As is customary in such cases, other Amazon users took up pitchforks and stormed Garadget's Amazon page to show solidarity with Martin, review-bombing the product.

Analysis of the circumstances showed that the manufacturer was primarily developing apps and decided to jump into IoT to push out his app more than anything else. As such, there was no tech support for users, who had to rely on community forums or just plain experimenting with the device to make it work. The device itself relied on cloud servers to do its function, which meant it constantly phoned home. This was also a crucial vulnerability in the design as

---

[12]https://arstechnica.com/information-technology/2017/04/iot-garage-door-opener-maker-bricks-customers-product-after-bad-review/

the developer could cut off any given user for any given reason from the servers. Luckily, Martin bought Garadget off of Amazon, and he could ask for a refund but what would've happened if he'd bought it directly from the developer?

IoT devices will require a sizable expansion of the infrastructure, meaning servers to crunch the data and produce a conclusion. This will mean an expansion of existing internet address space to accommodate the burgeoning number of devices. Right now, the internet is on IPv4, which uses 32-bit numbering and provides 4,294,967,296 (2^{32}) addresses. The proposed upgrade that's meant to provide more than enough addresses is IPv6, which uses 128-bit numbering to provide 340,282,366,920,938,463,463,374,607,431,768,211,456 (2^{128}) addresses. The number is read as 340 *undecillions* in the US (340 *sextillions* in the rest of the world). Now there's a couple of fun words to start the day off. But, who in their right mind would need that many IP addresses?

Chapter 4 – Internet of Things

In the US, IoT spending is mostly driven by government agencies, in particular, the Department of Homeland Security and NASA, which are working on sensors on munitions and related projects. A report by Govini[13], a company focused on providing federal agencies in the US with aggregate data needed to establish long-term policies, shows that federal spending for IoT sensors alone has nearly tripled between 2011-2015, going from $578MM to $1.6bn.

Military applications involve sensors on blimps to watch over supply lines and on tethered balloons to spot incoming threats. These systems were already tested in Iraq and Afghanistan, with the idea that they'll eventually be adapted for domestic and civilian use, such as to protect the US-Mexico border against illegal immigrants. NASA is working with universities to bring IoT sensors to areas such as healthcare, with products such as medical wearables that

---

[13]https://fcw.com/articles/2016/05/27/govini-iot-report.aspx

automatically test the blood sugar level of people with diabetes without drawing blood.

General Services Administration (GSA) is an independent US government body assigned to the task of managing the operation of federal agencies at a fundamental level. GSA manages some 10,000 government buildings across the nation and in 2013 decided to trial an IoT initiative called GSALink in 81 of them[14]. 13,000 sensors were embedded in trial properties, generating 27 million data points each day. Employees cooperate with GSALink by digitally registering their workspace and working wherever suits them, with lights and air conditioning managed automatically as people move through the building. For example, if a meeting is scheduled at a certain conference room, GSALink will automatically turn on the air conditioning a few hours prior and turn it off when the meeting ends. If an employee doesn't like the air temperature, he can ask GSALink to change it, at which point the system will query nearby employees and get an average of their votes before changing anything.

While GSALink does give hope in that the federal government will finally get something done better than the civilian sector, there's looming danger from overly broad adoption of IoT before clear guidelines have been adopted. A 2017 report[15] issued by the US Government Accountability Office lists the potential ways an IoT device could be compromised. Supply chain sabotage would come through the manufacturer of the device or its software embedding a malicious feature that would leave the device vulnerable. At best, the device will passively collect data; at worst, it will be used to hack into networks.

Limited encryption and transmission of viewable data is another problem since a hacker wouldn't need any access to the IoT device but simply a position somewhere on the intermediary network to

---

[14]https://www.fedscoop.com/mobile-gsalink

[15]https://www.gao.gov/assets/690/686203.pdf

scoop up the data. IoT devices typically don't use encryption to save on costs and time-to-market. Poorly implemented hardware features leading to little or no cybersecurity would be another weakness of IoT. Again, IoT devices aren't meant to withstand hacking attacks or any kind of adversarial behavior.

Poor default passwords can lead to wide-scale security breaches while a lack of upgrade or patching potential could cause a situation where an IoT network isn't patchable at all. Unpatched devices will remain functional despite being outdated, just like regular computers, which will be a source of temptation just to ignore any vulnerabilities. Rogue applications can be installed on IoT devices by careless users, gathering classified or private data for the benefit of commercial companies. Once data leaves containment, there's typically no way to know who else got it and what was done with it.

IoT wearables can track the geographical location of personnel and report their location to create a detailed schematic of patrol routes or classified facilities. This already happened with Strava's smartphone app intended for runners and cyclists to measure their progress that inadvertently showed locations of facilities[16] in Antarctica[17] and other remote locations.

The US Department of Defense has already claimed a chunk of the entire IPv6 namespace, namely 42 decillion[18] or about 0.01% of all IPv6 addresses. One reason for this could be security through obscurity – the idea being that all government agencies' servers can hide themselves in the proverbial haystack the size of the Solar System. Right now, it's fairly easy for any remote attacker to scan through IPv4 addresses to find entry points and just keep trying until

---

[16]https://www.strava.com/heatmap#11.50/-82.80919/-79.76416/hot/all

[17]https://www.strava.com/heatmap#13.52/11.62016/-70.82436/hot/all

[18]https://royal.pingdom.com/2009/03/26/the-us-department-of-defense-has-42-million-billion-billion-billion-ipv6-addresses/

he or she gets in, with the defender having to invest resources to secure his or her systems against intrusion actively.

Hacking attacks are precisely dangerous because it's impractical to defend against them; as new features and hardware are grafted onto the underlying infrastructure, the possibility of unintended interactions that cause a glitch or a bug increases dramatically. At some point, there comes a time for a paradigm shift, which would, in this case, be switching over to IPv6. Still, hackers will get some spiffy tools of their own in the form of quantum computers.

Digital technology we currently use revolves around magnetism and specks of magnetic charge representing 0s and 1s on hard disks to store data. As years went by, we got better and better at storing tinier specks on hard disks, meaning we now have storage of several terabytes on a device the size of a piece of toast. However, there are some problems with this approach. The hardware we have cannot properly scale, meaning there's a soft limit as to how many computers we can stack on top of one another and expect it to keep solving bigger and bigger problems, such as being able to model Earth's atmosphere accurately.

Another issue is the hard limit as to how small a speck of magnetic charge can be before it randomly dissipates, meaning the data is suddenly lost, at which point the hard disk is no longer a reliable device. This limit represents a strong barrier against further miniaturization. Prior to asking questions we can't answer, or making devices that randomly fail in a desperate attempt to answer them, we should start thinking about a replacement for magnetism in computing, which is atomic bits of data known as "quants" or "qubits".

The quantum world is a really bizarre one. It underlies our regular world full of chairs, bottles, and chandeliers, but expected rules of cause and effect that apply to those, don't apply there. For example, in the quantum world, there's a rule known as "entanglement" that states two particles may become joined for some reason and then instantly affect one another over arbitrarily long distances. So, shaking a quantum chandelier in Tokyo may instantly break a quantum chair in Austin, Texas and fill a quantum water bottle in Antarctica. There's very little logic to how quants interact, but scientists are desperate for any sort of paradigm shift that would help them answer burning questions about the nature of the world. What could possibly go wrong?

Quantum computers are, for now, only minute experiments used to regale the public and let scientists endlessly theorize, as through IBM's Q Experience. When we do get working quantum computers, in theory, they will fit the head of a pin and be able to crack any cryptography and search through the entire IPv6 namespace in a reasonable amount of time. With such inconceivable computing power, programmers might finally be able to create an actual AI, a thinking machine brain that could fit the space of a human cranium. Its theoretical capabilities are shrouded in mystery, but it would conceivably be at least on par with its creators – if not several degrees of magnitude smarter. Until then, we're left to use what little computing power we can cram into tiny IoT devices to produce things such as:

A smart toilet with ambient lighting and speakers for total immersion

News about Kohler's smart toilet dropped with a splash at the annual 2019 Consumer Electronics Show (CES) in Las Vegas, Nevada. Produced by a respectable plumbing company, Numi 2.0[19] is an intelligent toilet that can set the mood lighting and respond to voice commands using Alexa for a hands-free toilet experience worthy of a king. There's a separate seat-warming add-on too, but the main gimmick is having Numi work together with smart mirrors, a smart bathtub, and a smart shower, all produced by Kohler, so you can stay

---

[19]https://www.theverge.com/2019/1/6/18170575/kohler-konnect-bathroom-smart-gadgets-numi-intelligent-toilet-ces-2019

squeaky clean without ever letting go of your smartphone. The price for Numi 2.0 is $7,000 ($9,000 for a jet-black version).

A smart fishing rod for gathering stats on the spot

Among companies angling for attention at the 2019 CES was Cyber Fishing[20], presenting its Smart Fishing Rod to the audience. Well, what's wrong with a regular fishing rod? It can't record stats or locations of best catches, forcing the hapless fisher to write down the best spots or, God forbid, memorize them. The Smart Sensor is at the core of the Smart Fishing Rod, automatically capturing all the relevant data and letting the user easily share it online with others for fishing spots crowdsourcing. The downside is – there's no way to entertain the guys with exaggerated fishing tales.

A smart air purifier that moves around the house

Finally, you can breathe a sigh of relief through Atmobot[21], an Ecovacs autonomous air purifier teased at CES 2019 that looks like a trash can. It moves from room to room to purify the air and vacuum the carpet, with an optional array of fixture sensors sold separately to help Atmobot detect when the air gets bad to move there on its own. Deebot is Atmobot's younger sister that simply cleans the floor with in-built support for voice controls and a detachable mopping sponge. The previous version of Deebot was priced at AU$999 and tended to get stuck on carpets and cables[22].

A smart water faucet with LED lighting

In the age of IoT, you can't even drink a glass of water without a smartphone app. Tern Water[23] offers a "smart water faucet" that ties

---

[20] https://cyberfishing.com/

[21] https://www.pcworld.idg.com.au/article/656208/ces-2019-ecovacs-unveil-air-purifier-atmobot-upgraded-deebot/

[22] https://www.pcworld.idg.com.au/review/ecovacs/deebot-900-ozmo/646302/

[23] https://www.ternwater.com/

together with the app to warn the owner when the filter is about to expire or that there are contaminants in the pipes. The entire kit is $250, but the trick is that there's a monthly subscription service for whatever reason. The tap does have a cool LED indicator but also houses a battery that lasts up to one year.

Smart scented candles with the scent of money set on fire

Moodo[24] is a palm-sized box that fits four fragrance capsules lasting 60 hours. Of course, it's connected to a smartphone app that lets the owner adjust the aroma combination according to the app's mood meter or schedule scent release right as he or she is about to arrive home. You can also adjust Moodo halfway across the world – because why not? What's the catch? Moodo is about $160, and each capsule costs another 35. MoodoGo is the portable version for the car that goes into the lighter port.

Smart farms

In what is most certainly bullish news, Australian farmers have been trying to incorporate IoT into their work and digitize everything from cows to fences[25]. Unreliable connectivity and data quotas torpedoed these ambitious plans, and one of these farmers said, "We can't apply [IoT] in 90% of situations." A conglomerate of grazing businesses spread over 6,000 hectares, Carwool Pastoral, deployed over 200 IoT devices and found only a handful, such as smoke alarms, cattle tags, silo level monitors and shed condition monitors, had any appreciable use. Even when devices did work, the wilderness was so poorly covered with internet reception that farmers couldn't rely on any IoT device that required the internet to function. To make matters worse each IoT device came with a separate app, and app developers had no intention of cooperating or

---

[24]https://moodo.co/what-is-moodo/

[25]https://www.itnews.com.au/news/australian-farmers-are-battling-to-make-iot-work-516204

combining their data into a single stream to make the farmers' lives easier; imagine juggling 55 apps to check on your farmstead.

Smart sprinklers that can be turned on and off from halfway across the world

Named Sprinkl[26], this set of IoT sprinkler modules eliminates any need for human oversight, but at what price? With Alexa-controlled interface and priced at $225, Control SR-400 represents the sprinkler hub that requires a Wi-Fi connection to work, with the only flaw that it has to control sixteen zones or more. Sprinkl requires smart sensors Sense SR-100, one per zone and each costing $45. Another Sprinkl module is Conserve SR-301, priced at $79, that adds smartphone control to sprinklers, marketed as "turn off the sprinklers from your phone anywhere in the world." The total cost for all three modules is at least $1,024. So, is there any actual benefit to having the possibility to turn your sprinklers on and off halfway across the world?

A smart block of wood

You thought it was a joke, didn't you? It's almost zen-like with the artistic flair that defies belief – just a block of wood and the internet. Now presenting Mui, a smart home hub that has been described as "an elegant device" and is meant to mimic the woody look of furniture. It's essentially a narrow plank with electronics embedded inside that's hung on the wall and shows essential information, such as thermostat temperature. There's a display panel on Mui, but the material is actual wood coming from Japanese Hida forest. Mui already got $115,000 out of required $100,000 on Kickstarter[27] and should be delivered sometime at the start of 2019, priced at $549 for backers and $999 in retail.

---

[26]https://sprinkl.com/

[27]https://www.kickstarter.com/projects/1391686171/mui-interactive-wood-panel-for-peaceful-digital-li

A smart padlock

Dubbed "the world's worst padlock" and described as "it's EVEN WORSE than we thought" by security firm Sophos[28], Tapplock is a product of a Canadian IoT company that decided to create its own cryptographic protection scheme. Bluetooth-enabled padlock with a fingerprint scanner, Tapplock has a fatal flaw – knowing the network address of the padlock is enough to crack its cryptographic protection. Since network addresses are meant to be broadcast publicly, the result was anyone who wanted to take a look could easily crack Tapplock, which another security firm did by making a program that performed the hack in two seconds straight. Priced at $99, Tapplock turned out to be completely hackable even remotely, without any physical access to the device, but also helpfully revealed the location of the padlock so the hacker could go waltz right in and pick up whatever valuables it was meant to guard. These vulnerabilities have been patched.

A smart menstrual cup

Small, disposable and utterly hackable, IoT devices have shown themselves insecure over and over again. So why not put one inside your own body? Looncup[29] is literally at the bleeding edge of IoT development, as it's a smart menstrual cup that connects to a smartphone app using Bluetooth to show information, such as how full the cup is. There's a non-replaceable, non-rechargeable battery embedded in Looncup's silicone, meaning it can last a couple of months, after which it will serve as a regular menstrual cup. Additional functions include scanning the color of the blood for health problems and tracking the menstrual cycle. Like many other low-key IoT projects, Looncup began on Kickstarter.

---

[28]https://nakedsecurity.sophos.com/2018/06/18/the-worlds-worst-smart-padlock-its-even-worse-than-we-thought/

[29]https://www.looncup.com/

Entrepreneurs are capitalizing on IoT hype by just making whatever seemed like a cool idea, but what about third world governments? There's an interesting aspect of IoT as it can help city officials manage affairs. So, what if we built cities with IoT in mind?

Smart cities

In a first world environment, IoT devices represent a luxury, such as smart doorbells and toilets, but in third world countries, smart-city systems made of IoT devices might actually become a fundamental part of the infrastructure. Mumbai is one of many Indian metropolises, housing 20 million residents that all want to ride one of city's 3 million cars or rickshaws to and from work. When monsoon season hits, usually lasting from June through August, Mumbai experiences a total traffic collapse.

With the help of IoT devices, such as traffic sensors, the local government can redirect traffic to less-used roads and at least try to assuage traffic jams. Other problems, such as sewage management, can also be approached with IoT to get a glimpse into major population trends. Mumbai, not San Francisco or New York, is thus en route to becoming the first smart city powered by metrics gathered through IoT. With population growth and the gradual collapse of local governments, especially when it comes to traffic, we might see more and more reliance on IoT to gather data and neural networks or AI to make relevant decisions. Simply put: humans can't handle governing themselves in such large cities.

Having IoT sensors on garbage bins can tell sanitation workers when they should go on a patrol and which route is the most efficient rather than them having a fixed schedule that might not reverberate with, say, people throwing out more garbage during holidays. In this way, waste flows into landfills and recycle plants in a steady and more controlled manner.

IoT thermostats could automatically reduce heating in those areas where nobody is spending any time, and IoT lightbulbs could automatically dim and brighten as people walk through rooms to save power. IoT traffic lights could adjust to traffic conditions ahead and IoT sensors on parking spots could interact with digital maps, such as Google Maps, to provide useful information on nearby parking spots. IoT sensors embedded in asphalt could report wear and tear before potholes form.

The major issue with this Utopian vision of a smart city that runs itself is the lack of standards among IoT manufacturers and programmers. Everyone does things his or her way, and it's as if apps are intentionally made to conflict with one another. Lack of standards is a common sore point when it comes to software, with each developer stubbornly refusing to adapt or cooperate with his or her competition. As software companies rise to prominence and wane away, the consumer market is peppered with proprietary formats and designs that become useless after official support ends.

It took us decades of anguished struggle between software developers to arrive at having PDF and MP3 formats that are universally recognized across all mobile and desktop devices; intermediary file formats were used for a little bit and quickly forgotten. Applied to IoT, this means we can likely expect an explosion in experimentation with regards to designs and formats until the entire world settles on a couple of solid standards after a few decades. Of course, early adopters will get shafted, but the prospects of a smart city are so tantalizing.

Ideally, one overarching AI could finely control the environment throughout the entire city, cutting down on passive losses common to all power and heating distribution systems. A fleet of drones could be sent out automatically to clean up and scrub after a festival or public party was held. By analyzing behavior patterns, AI could know who's about to get sick and what's the effective treatment *before* the person feels the first symptoms. IoT devices in our homes would act as alarms and notifiers – ever had that overwhelming fear you left the stove on? IoT could be connected to heat sensors in appliances that would buzz your smartphone if you actually did.

That's the ideal future, but what we're looking at is mostly a chaotic array of gadgets cool in design but barely functional because they refuse to work together. If Samsung does waste disposal, Google does heating, and Apple does power supply, the three might intentionally sabotage one another, but if Samsung does *all three* in one city, now we're getting the coherence IoT gadgets need to function as a part of a broader network.

What are the implications for the democratic process in one such city where a company essentially has insight in all consumption and behavior patterns of the population? Can you criticize Samsung in Samsungville? How trustworthy are elected officials that kowtow to tech giants? Can we even escape the influence of tech giants?

Chapter 5 – Under The Cushy Foot of Tech Giants

Those who tried cutting tech giants out of their personal and work life experienced a swift and humiliating defeat. In January 2019, a Gizmodo journalist tried to cut out five tech giants for a week each, with the third week dedicated to Google[30]. After setting up VPN filters that blocked Google's IPs for her devices, the journalist was essentially unable to do any work and couldn't even use Uber or Lyft, as they engage Google Maps to operate correctly. Spotify hosts its content on Google's cloud, so no music either; AirBnB dumps its photos there as well, so they didn't load. Fonts, analytics and just random tidbits of code are all helpfully hosted by Google, which means the websites she used were acting up in all sorts of unusual ways. In short, her browsing experience was like being back in the early 90s: slow, messy and barely usable.

---

[30] https://gizmodo.com/i-cut-google-out-of-my-life-it-screwed-up-everything-1830565500

Eventually, we might all be living under a cushy foot of tech giants to the point that trying to get out will be too uncomfortable. Bit by bit, who we are and what we do is being pinned down to the point where we can't keep any secrets, shifting our life to the cloud where tech companies have supreme control of our activities. Arcane rules of conduct and vague terms of service already dominate on social media platforms, where accounts can get suspended for satirical content that others share freely. In some cases, tech companies can even decide to enforce rules of conduct *off their platform*.

In late 2018, the crowdfunding platform Patreon decided to ban a user[31], a certain Carl Benjamin, for comments he made on YouTube, despite Patreon's terms of service never mentioning or implying that option. This would apparently open Patreon to lawsuits for breach of contract, which is what terms of service legally represent, but so far none of those have materialized. Instead, users voted with their feet and left the website in search of better options only to find that, well, there aren't any. So, Patreon is a minnow website dedicated to a niche audience. What does one do if Google decides to enforce its terms of service for an off-hand comment made in real life and comprehensively de-platform an individual? It's actually impossible to punish Google in any significant way without destroying the internet as we know it.

There are simply no enshrined rights for individuals online like there are in the real world through constitutional charters, yet we sorely need to have them formulated. The same way our societies went through tumultuous times where whimsical tyrants lashed out at citizenry before evolving to democratic cultures that respect human dignity, we need to have our online world evolve *before* IoT becomes a staple. We needed to have them *yesterday*, or technological progress will become just another outlet for whimsical tyrants to feed their ego. Power truly does corrupt, and when tech

---

[31]https://www.businessinsider.com/patreon-crowdfunding-platform-defends-itself-amid-boycott-2018-12

giants wield so much power that they can undo a person from the internet, they kind of lose sight of reality.

Google, Amazon and other tech giants thus become 500-pound gorillas that sit in our home and occasionally lend a hand to do the heavy lifting – just keep your head down and don't look them in the eye or they'll kick you out. When other, smaller gorillas see we're not putting up a fight, they'll move in too, and our home will become a circus rather than a sanctified resting spot. There doesn't seem to be any pushback to this encroachment, and the media is disinterested in headlines that involve a thoughtful debate about such an abstract issue; today's media is all about clickbait, meaning titles that attract clicks and push copies at newsstands.

The best protection we can employ is to fragment our online persona as much as possible, meaning we should separate all our accounts so banning any of them doesn't collapse our entire digital identity. So, you could be "Karl" on YouTube, Karl123 on Yahoo, Karl234 on Amazon and so on. The more you can separate between your online accounts, the more you are shielded from the tyranny of tech companies. Yes, this does mean remembering a dozen or so very strong passwords and constantly logging in and out of accounts, but that's the price of freedom of speech and thought. If possible, try to have a dedicated device for each service: a smartphone only for YouTube, a laptop only for Yahoo, a tablet only for Amazon, and so on.

The trite argument of "just don't use the website if you don't like it" sort of works because the individual can still go in the real world and do something else. What happens when IoT makes everything connected to the internet, and there's no escape from denial of service? Fine, so we'll make an alternative to Google – we'll make a company that cherishes freedom of speech and honors terms of service. Any competitor to Google can be blocked from Google services, which would include marking that person's website as malicious, removing his or her app from Google Play, removing related search results from Google Search and denying him or her access to Google Cloud storage. It's effectively as if being unpersoned and completely erased from existence in the digital age.

When tech giants go mad gorilla against one another is when we pull out some popcorn and enjoy the carnage. January 29, 2019, is when Apple discovered that Facebook was abusing its enterprise privileges and blocked all Facebook apps from functioning off of Apple's cloud for two days[32]. Facebook employees experienced the same effect as that Gizmodo journalist – they couldn't even check their calendars or schedule a lunch because all of their infrastructure was hosted on Apple cloud.

What happened was that Facebook enlisted teenagers, as young as thirteen, through ads and had them install a **VPN**, a virtual private network that filters traffic, using an app that intercepted and scanned their internet traffic for some $20 in gift cards. This was against all imaginable privacy policies and was likely illegal too. In June 2018, one Facebook app, Onavo Protect, that did the same thing and was already banned by Apple, then updated its developer policy to stop such abuse from happening again. This time, the app was codenamed Project Atlas, but journalists that peeked inside the app's code found numerous references to Onavo Protect, confirming that the spying project was simply renamed.

For two days, the Apple cloud was inaccessible to Facebook, making much of its internal work impossible. After that, Facebook was allowed back in, despite doing what would have made some other developer permanently banned from Apple cloud. That's simply the kind of influence tech giants wield that allows them to create their bubble of sovereignty where they can ignore laws and bypass all rules and morals. So, what happens if an upstart company decides to offer an alternative? It simply gets bought off.

---

[32]https://techcrunch.com/2019/01/29/facebook-project-atlas/

Chapter 6 – The Power of Infinite Funds

Onavo Protect was initially a VPN app that helped users stop ads and trackers that hogged their bandwidth, but Facebook acquired the company in 2014 for some $120MM. Because user data is considered an asset of the company, by acquiring Onavo, Facebook got all the data that users thought would be kept private. Seeing how Facebook made some $50bn in 2018, $120MM was chump change, but Onavo executives were most likely ecstatic because they got to live the dream of cashing out and spending their retirement in the Bahamas. There was no way for Onavo to resist the buy-off since executives are supposed to do whatever isn't strictly illegal that will make the company money; had a moral Onavo executive decided he didn't want to sell, the rest of the board would have had to relieve him prior to selling the company anyway.

Buying Onavo let Facebook essentially spy on its users, which showed a certain app was being used much more than Facebook's Messenger – WhatsApp. Facebook jumped in and bought WhatsApp for $19bn, which was and still is the largest acquisition of a company in history. The motivation for buying WhatsApp was to create a sort of umbrella network of free essential services, such as Facebook for organizing social events, WhatsApp for messaging, and so on. Dubbed "internet.org", the app intended to deliver these services was named Free Basics in 2015 and was aimed at the poorest nations, India in particular. It's too bad India banned Free Basics, stating it had discriminatory tariffs.

So, if Facebook offered free services, how was it going to foot the bill? With users' private data. By making itself the gatekeeper of internet services for people too poor to afford a non-spying alternative, Facebook wanted to reach an unprecedented level of insight and control over its users, who would have nowhere else to go. The trick is to rope in children as early as possible and hook them into using social services through Facebook's funnel, which is why Project Atlas was intentionally aimed at the youngest teens possible – a company that can hook kids into its ecosystem of products basically has them for life. This is the strategy of soda makers, breakfast cereal producers and other such companies that deal with products that provide immediate gratification.

There are no protections that would aim specifically at protecting private data of children, who often have no concept of social norms and tend to say stupid things. Despite everyone taking up arms whenever children are endangered, this doesn't seem to apply to persistent, low-key threats but only dramatic and explosive ones, as explained in "Freakonomics"[33]; children are constantly warned about the dangers of guns but never about the dangers of swimming pools, which are statistically much deadlier but aren't as violent.

Prior to the internet becoming widespread, children had the luxury to be obnoxious and inane, with only their immediate surroundings knowing about it. Thanks to social media, their stupidity can now

---

[33]https://www.amazon.com/Freakonomics-Revised-Expanded-Economist-Everything/dp/0061234001

follow them their entire life, impacting their employment and relationships decades in the future. Of course, companies have not an inkling of concern about this – since they only want to make money and "make the world a better place". In any case, the initial discovery that Facebook was using Onavo Protect to leech data was what prompted Apple to tighten up its developer privacy policy. Google was found using a similar scheme[34] to leech data from teens but abruptly ended the program when journalists asked about it. When the same corporate logic is applied to toys is when things take a more sinister turn.

---

[34] https://techcrunch.com/2019/01/30/googles-also-peddling-a-data-collector-through-apples-back-door/

Chapter 7 – IoT Toys

When applied to toys, IoT becomes a terrifying tool of surveillance, even when done unintentionally and out of negligence. Children's most intimate moments with their parents become open to any scoundrel who might want to listen in to their conversations or scammers who might want to blackmail the company. In one such case, IoT teddy bears were found to be storing all recorded messages and profile info in a public-facing database.

Marketed as "A Message You Can Hug," CloudPets is a collection of teddy bears and other plush toys that can record and transmit voice messages between kids and their parents. The only problem was – all personal data related to CloudPets was stored in a public database that was accessible online by anyone who wanted to spend a few minutes looking for it. In February 2017, word got out to Troy Hunt, an Australian cybersecurity researcher who at one point testified in front of the US Congress on data breaches, so he took a peek[35] and was stunned at how bad the security was.

---

[35] https://www.troyhunt.com/data-from-connected-cloudpets-teddy-bears-leaked-and-ransomed-exposing-kids-voice-messages/

CloudPets had over 2 million voice messages belonging to about 820,000 owners stored online to cut on costs and engineering complexity needed to make the toy itself store messages, which would be the safest thing to do. E-mail addresses and encrypted passwords were stored in MongoDB, an open source database that uses an easily copyable text format rather than rows and columns like Excel. Contacting the owner of CloudPets via e-mail about the vulnerability produced no reply; apparently, there was nobody at the wheel.

Troy then analyzed CloudPets' app behavior and discovered that it stored profiles on Amazon servers, containing profile photos, names of kids, dates of birth and their relationship to the adult that bought them the toy. Recordings of kids' messages could be accessed by simply knowing the file path to them on the server, which Troy tested out and actually heard a few of them. Weak passwords were another headache, with the official CloudPets tutorial showing account creation that included using a mere three-character password. Troy tested the stored passwords using a dictionary attack and found plenty of them being "12345", "password" and other such easily hackable ones.

In other words, there was no requirement for a password to be of any particular length or complexity; one could put a single character as a CloudPets password. Once a password is found, there's an associated e-mail address displayed right next to it in the database, so the hacker can simply log in as a legitimate user to the given CloudPets account.

Hackers didn't stop merely at listening to lovely audio messages; they actually deleted the exposed databases and replaced them with ransom messages stating that a backup could be retrieved for one Bitcoin, which was about $1,000 at the time. An e-mail address attached to the ransom note indicated the hackers were from India, but none of that mattered because there was still no official reply. The owner company experienced a 99% drop in stock price since releasing CloudPets, resulting in downsizing that likely took out all tech support and interest in maintaining the product line.

The reply by Californian-based CloudPets CEO, Mark Meyers, was that those voice recordings were not stolen, that headlines of 2 million messages being leaked online were false, and that the security weaknesses were a "very minimal issue." Technically, he *is* correct, but what about addressing the underlying problems? When asked about not having password strength requirements, Mark replied, "How much is too much?" When asked about the warnings, Mark said that it's their policy to ignore warnings coming from random people, indicating that a security issue is only a big deal if it's about to appear in nationwide publications.

Troy's advice with buying and using IoT toys is to "assume breach" – meaning that you should consider security non-existent unless proven otherwise. This means that it's up to you to discover and change default settings (if any), set a strong password, and otherwise discover how the device works before handing it off to the kid or merely bringing it inside your home. For busy parents who think IoT toys will help them save time, it's quite the contrary – now they've got to learn the essentials of cybersecurity and networking or risk all their personal information being exposed to unsavory characters.

CloudPets' story is one of few where someone with expertise cared enough to take a look, analyze the situation, and write up a report; otherwise, none of it would have ever come out to the public. For CEOs that produce IoT toys, each sale is relevant insofar as it generates revenue; products and services become a liability that needs to be minimized and ignored whenever possible. CloudPets' CEO response is the perfect example of how to slyly handle a security incident with rhetorical questions, dismissals, and vague explanations. Unless we as consumers start taking care with ours and our children's security in a world filled with IoT, nobody will.

In the hands of hackers, all IoT devices become toys, as it were. The more we scale up IoT without addressing these fundamental security issues, the more we'll be exposing ourselves and our loved ones to endangerment. It's quite possible that the way we imagine IoT right now isn't feasible on a worldwide scale, but can only work locally. We're simply stumped for answers. Perhaps the solution is to wear personalized IoT sensors and have IoT access points inside a house or workplace reading movement, speech, mood, and behavior. But again – can it scale?

The same way a tiny flea can jump a foot in the air but wouldn't be able to move if it were scaled up because the materials it's made out of wouldn't be strong enough, some systems only work when done on a tiny scale, and it appears IoT is one of these. Fragmentation and localization of IoT networks take the wind out of the sails of most IoT marketing strategies that would ideally want everything to become IoT – of course, with proprietary hardware and software. So, if IoT vendors use third-party open standard software, what's the risk a single exploit or bug can bring the entire network down?

Security firm Senrio conceptualized an attack called **Devil's Ivy**, where a bug found in the third-party code used in IoT devices can be exploited to compromise devices themselves. With Devil's Ivy, the focus is on gSOAP, a C++ framework used to develop **SOAP**, Simple Object Access Protocol, which is meant to unify different IoT operating systems and frameworks through XML. Basically, two IoT devices using SOAP can communicate as long as there's an internet connection between them no matter what their manufacturer or operating system. It sounds great – for hackers that is.

Devil's Ivy allows a hacker to exploit a bug in SOAP found on an IoT device, such as a CCTV camera, by sending a malicious 2GB payload that overflows the device and resets it to factory settings. Then, the hacker logs into the device and can either try to access other vulnerable devices or just quietly absorb information by looking over the shoulders of employees as they're typing in their passwords. If a router is hacked this way, the hacker just got access to all network traffic, which is as good as full access to all devices on that network. By the time the owners spot a problem, *and* the device vendor issues a patch, hackers could've been spying on people for decades.

The company that made SOAP, Genivia, issued a patch for that particular bug while noting at least 34 IoT vendors use SOAP. What happens if a commonly used IoT framework is found weak at some point in time, but there's no central authority to issue a patch? Who can force companies to patch their IoT products if that comes at a cost? Right now, the only advocates for IoT standards are non-profits.

The Open Connectivity Foundation[36] (OCF) is a valiant effort to create IoT security and connectivity standards by advocating for "security by design", meaning hardware and software is built in expectation of being hacked. Pushing for this concept is in a sense a way to preemptively quash all complaints from companies that security is expensive; by baking security into initial design, all costs are offset onto customers. OCF also aims to create a model for centralized IoT management using public keys infrastructure, meaning a company can update all its IoT products in one go.

It sounds great, and it makes a juicy article headline, but it's unlikely to happen. Companies are typically prone to what's known as "virtue signaling", where executives say whatever makes them look good but do the most selfish thing anyway. This is why every Silicon Valley executive, such as Apple's Tim Cook, spouts exuberant phrases in the vein of "Apple makes the world a better place"[37]; Apple will then allow Facebook to collect teenager data using Apple Cloud. If tech giants are dominating the digital world, at least we have the real world – where we can go outside and enjoy nature without IoT, right?

---

[36]https://openconnectivity.org/blog/iot-security-design

[37]https://youtu.be/glFLpkCnSPU?t=237

Chapter 8 – Bio-robotics

It's one thing to be surrounded by IoT indoors because you can simply step out for some privacy, but it's something quite different when IoT gets deployed outdoors as well. If there's a commercial application to outdoors IoT deployment, you can be sure that it's going to get done one way or another.

IoT devices enable real-time collection of granular data to visualize complex environments through the mass movement of individual units. One such IoT concept imagines bumblebees as "living platforms" for IoT sensors. In "Living IoT: A Flying Wireless Platform on Live Insects"[38], five researchers from the University of Washington imagined a world where bumblebees equipped with IoT sensors help humans do what they termed **bio-robotics**, grafting of digital devices on analog beings. It's actually quite a practical approach that solves many insurmountable problems.

---

[38] http://livingiot.cs.washington.edu/files/livingiot.pdf

Engineering a drone to serve as a mobile IoT platform comes with many headaches, such as design, energy source, wingspan, miniaturization and getting funds for all that. Living insects are an example of living perfection, so simply tacking lightweight IoT sensors on them essentially hacks all those problems in one fell swoop. Bumblebees are extremely efficient in gathering resources and spending as few of them as possible for their operations, again making them a great surrogate for IoT drones. They also have navigation down to a T with innate magnetic sensors that help them align with the Earth's magnetic field, hence why we say "beeline" for a perfectly straight line.

Weighing 0.1g, the sensor carried by the bumblebee can be detected within 80m of the nearest access point and can transmit 1kbps of data when the insect is back at the hive. The battery on board the bumblebee lasts up to seven hours while recording the current location fifteen times a minute. With alternative sensor modules for humidity, temperature, and light, a swarm of bumblebees can be turned into an efficient mapping tool to find out the most suitable location for any given plant that requires a certain combination of humidity, temperature, and light to thrive.

A suggestion presented in the paper is surgically inserting IoT sensors into bumblebees at various stages of their development. The electronic waste would become an issue, but the IoT sensors could be built to transmit the location as the insect is expiring and biodegradable sensors are a possibility. Conceivably, there could be a fleet of slightly larger IoT drones designed to go around and clean up dead IoT bumblebees, a fleet of even larger drones for picking those up, and so on. It would be drones all the way up, but would that make the world a better place?

The main limitation in IoT drone manufacturing is battery life. Currently, the most efficient batteries use lithium, which is thought to be the lightest material possible for storing energy. As scientists tweak the lithium formula, it's possible they'll find ways to squeeze a bit more power out of battery design, but then the progress inevitably plateaus; unless there's a paradigm shift past that, we'll be stuck with lithium batteries for the rest of the future. In comparison, bumblebees use macronutrients – proteins, fats, and carbohydrates – to power their operations. We use these three as well, simply because they're everywhere and provide lots of energy, just like fossil fuels.

As tempting as it may sound to ditch organic energy sources, we'll be stuck with them for the foreseeable future because they're relatively cheap, reliable and efficient, but they miniaturize poorly. Even electric cars run into the same problem of having to cart around bulky lithium batteries that need to recharge, which is mostly done by using the power created by burning fossil fuels. Right now, all IoT devices are merely stationary and semi-stationary appliances, so can we make IoT *wearable*? Apparently, the answer to that is a resounding "yes," and we might actually need wearable IoT to maintain our health and social well-being.

For children with autism, daily life is a constant struggle as they can regularly fail to do the most basic things, such as tying their shoelaces. Autism itself is a catch-all term for brain dysfunction that results in socially unacceptable behavior; there's no real boundary as to what is autistic, so the illness is seen on a spectrum. Such children lack a healthy emotional response to natural circumstances, such as feeling fear when they're in danger or speaking up when they're hurt and often find themselves ostracized. Because, normally, emotions would guide us to a better life, autistic children can experience tremendous stress that leads them to bottle it all up and then have emotional meltdowns for apparently no reason. In any case, IoT wearables can really help children with autism get a grip on reality, but especially help their parent keep their sanity.

Now here's where Google Glass and the cohort of analytic eyewear could help – this is worn by people who truly can't discern emotions on the faces of people they're interacting with, such as autistic kids talking to their parents. Because the environment is trusted and there's actual productivity lost due to inability to see emotions, there's a strong incentive to use IoT. However, what do we do if the parent can't understand their autistic child either?

In this case, an IoT bracelet serves to track the child's reaction to the environment and report the findings, perhaps to a parent's smartphone app. By monitoring the heart rate, a parent can see when the child is experiencing stress and can react straight away instead of waiting for the meltdown. How will the parent know what to do? Whatever causes the child's heart rate to slow down is what it takes to calm the kid. These bracelets are similar to those worn by fitness enthusiasts: simple, sturdy and effective.

Smart bracelets can be used by people with diabetes to scan for blood sugar levels and determine if there's any need for a reaction without drawing blood. Diabetes is so insidious that it takes an entire network of people to keep just one person with diabetes in check. Nutritionists and doctors could have instant access to this information to schedule a checkup, especially in cases where the patient has trouble moving – which is again another common symptom of diabetes. Family members could also keep an eye out for blood sugar levels and intervene when needed with a meal or just a glass of orange juice. One such bracelet is already on the market, dubbed GlucoSentry[39]. Apple is already capitalizing on the medical wearables market with its smartwatch that can track health signals and possibly report them to a medical professional.

As technology advances, we on average have a longer lifespan, which means more chronic health problems, such as cancer and diabetes. Medicine is suffering tremendous costs with simply keeping these patients alive, so IoT wearables could help cut down costs without just hiring more people to do costly medical exams. In medicine, IoT could be indispensable because we're already struggling with the lack of specialized staff to draw blood, measure blood pressure, and so on. A doctor needs to have immediate results

---

[39]http://www.coolwearable.com/glucosentry-bracelet-diabetics/

to make the right call or risk being sued for malpractice, but there's the lack of staff, patient discomfort, and paperwork – IoT devices neatly fix all those problems and might even administer drugs automatically. For example, MiniMed 530G is an implantable pancreas that comes with an external sensor that shows blood sugar and insulin levels.

At the 2018 Medical Sensors Design conference held in San Jose, California, projected growth of medical wearables was said to be about $12bn by 2021. This includes masks[40] to exercise the facial muscles that might have degraded due to surgery or other causes but also monitors inserted in a woman's body to track ovulation.

OvulaRing is a smart ovulation monitor that tracks the core body temperature to report when an egg is released. It's already available in the European Union at $520 for a twelve-month package.

HealthPatch MD is a wearable sensor that looks like a nicotine patch. It detects body posture, heart rate, skin temperature, and respiratory rate while triggering an alert if the wearer too suddenly changes posture, which could indicate they've fallen.

Zio XT Patch is a heart rhythm monitoring patch that can be worn up to two weeks continuously, revealing abnormal heart activity patterns. Data is sent over to the app that then crunches it using algorithms.

Quell is a knee band that looks to reduce pain and discomfort, coordinating with the smartphone app via Bluetooth to squeeze and release as needed to massage the area.

WristOx2 is a watch-like wristband that monitors oxygen saturation in the blood and changes in blood volume in the skin.

The biggest obstacle to IoT medical wearables in the US is getting FDA approval, which can take years and hundreds of thousands of

---

[40] https://www.informationweek.com/healthcare/mobile-and-wireless/10-medical-device-wearables-to-improve-patients-lives/d/d-id/1323544

dollars in clinical trials. This is why Apple released a "smartwatch" that was met with ridicule for being too simplistic for its cost; Apple exploited a loophole that allowed it to sell medical tracking technology without FDA authorization under the guise of selling a watch. It's actually a brilliant business move. The big companies know how to monetize their fanbases, but they'll also be getting a wealth of data to analyze consumer behavior on a grand scale and predict their decisions, which is termed **predictive analytics**.

Chapter 9 – Predictive Analytics

Now that a company has access to data from sources such as IoT wearables, how can it be used for analysis? First, the data is *anonymized*, which means any personally identifiable information is removed. This neatly dodges wiretapping regulation but otherwise doesn't mean much because each data source is labeled with a number that can always be traced back to the person. By gathering all the data from as many different sources as possible, the algorithm or neural network at the other side weaves a digital doppelganger to the person and tries to predict their behavior. Wait, are we so predictable?

We all have an extremely basic part of the brain called the **limbic system** that houses essential urges and functions, such as hunger, aggression, and territoriality. It is extremely *fast* and efficient, acting before we get the chance to think about it consciously. When we observe the action of the limbic system, we often do it in hindsight and can't cope with the fact it's basically working on autopilot, so we assign it ulterior motives which aren't correct in the slightest, "I meant to do that all along!" However, a machine is a dispassionate observer and can see through the fog of rationalization to deliver the *truth* that can be seen by the entire world.

Companies generally keep the findings of their research locked away, but for the first time, IoT provides everyone with a chance to participate in this grand experiment *and* get the results. While it does feel like machine spies are violating our privacy, predictive analytics can help us understand our brain because *we have no idea how the human brain works*. In this way, machines reveal our behavior to us, and companies are already capitalizing on this concept. Simply put: we're the smartest creatures on the planet and can adapt to anything as long as we can see our behavior in an objective way, such as by using IoT wearable sensors.

Humanyze[41] touts itself as "science-backed analytics to improve your compliance." The team adjacencies metric gives each employee a rating on how good he or she is when communicating with his or her immediate team and the rest of the company. Both volume and gaps are taken into account to assess the communication risk each employee poses when it comes to the delivery of valuable work and expressed as percentages and hours.

Time allocation metric shows how each team member spends his or her time using a communication medium, broken down as chat, e-mail, phone call, and meeting. After work hours are included too, showing who's available after they leave work and revealing cultural differences that can be grafted onto other teams if needed. Periods go from one week to one year, but 'role' is the most important factor in assessing appropriateness. In the end, this metric can answer that one burning question, "Are we having too many meetings?"

Communication by gender metric measures the volume and type of communication sent by each employee and broken down by gender. In this way, gendered preferences to using any particular mode of

---

[41]https://www.humanyze.com/

communication are revealed, helping with better integration in the company – for example, if men or women are invited more or less often to meetings or called over the phone. The result of these metrics is a 2D graph that looks like a spider web and visualizes connections between team members.

Founded in 2010 by MIT students and one professor, Humanyze utilizes sociometric ID badges to track movement and performance, essentially giving employees wearable sensors that don't intrude on the communication or impart their opinion of the interactions taking place. Their 2008 paper "Understanding Organizational Behavior with Wearable Sensing Technology"[42] goes into greater detail on how each personal relationship consists of four basic behaviors that fundamentally predict productivity.

The badge form was chosen since employees are often already asked to wear ID badges; Humanyze badges were pimped out with microphones, infrared transceivers and accelerometers to show movement and speech patterns. Sturdy, easy to use and unobtrusive, the badge could recognize:

- if the wearer was sitting, walking, standing or running in real time
- analyze vocal tonality shifts to measure excitement and interjections while ignoring the words themselves (again, note the sly dodging of wiretapping laws)
- the position of each wearer through triangulation of the badge's position, with error as low as five feet (1.5 meters)
- nearby Bluetooth-enabled devices and communicate with them

---

[42]https://papers.ssrn.com/sol3/papers.cfm?abstract_id=1263992

- face-to-face interactions because the infrared sensors in badges could spot each other

One of the goals of the paper was to determine *interdependence*, meaning how much employees have to communicate with one another to complete any given task; if they are interdependent more than their communication skills allow, their productivity will suffer. So, the students and their professor went to a German bank with their badges and started gathering data.

Over the course of one month, 22 employees in the bank distributed as four teams, two mid-level managers and one high-level manager wore Humanyze badges while they were on the clock, resulting in 2,200 hours of data. Individual and group performance satisfaction was also measured through a survey at the end of each workday and e-mail logs were gathered as well. Employees were 50-50 men and women, though all managers were men. Employees were split across two floors, which was another reason why the bank was interested in Humanyze's view of things – does that layout impact our performance?

The results showed that the amount of time spent with other people negatively correlated with e-mail activity, which showed that e-mail *is not* a replacement for face-to-face contact. Further, the total amount of communication *lowered* the employee's satisfaction value, as self-reported through the daily survey. Bank layout did not impact employees negatively since only the managers interacted between floors and the key premise was that an employee that is central to an organization experiences lower satisfaction. Next up, the team visited a Chicago data server configuration firm.

Conditions of the second experiment were similar: one month and 23 employees wearing badges until 1,900 hours of data were collected. All were men but their skill levels varied. Their job consisted of waiting until a field salesman contacted them with client preferences regarding a computer configuration, at which point they would use a certain program to create that configuration and send it alongside the price estimate back to the salesman.

Four types of behavior were spotted: low/high physical activity with/without speaking. High physical activity was essentially fidgeting, which is the activation of the limbic system that wants to fight or flee when it feels cornered. Frequent speaking is another sign of the same limbic system activation. Both fidgeting and frequent speaking are indicators of stress, which is known to impact productivity negatively. So, researchers theorized that those employees with the least physical activity *and* who spent the least time speaking would be the most productive.

Findings confirmed that theory and showed that the low physical activity without speaking group did their tasks 63% *faster* than the high physical activity with speaking group. The number of follow-ups, which are repeated calls from the same salesman regarding the same configuration, was *28% lower* in the former group compared to the latter, implying the tasks were also done more precisely. The conclusion was that "environmental distraction in an individual may trigger bursts of activity, and this distraction subsequently lowers performance." The lesson from this would be – if you want to be efficient at your job, stop fidgeting and stay silent.

In 2011, Humanyze produced glasses that serve as a social cue detector[43]. When worn and looking at a person's face, these glasses use an attached headphone to explain what the other person is feeling, "Bored, disappointed". There is even a tiny traffic light embedded on the glasses frame that warns when the other person is about to speak, so the wearer doesn't interrupt. 24 facial points are analyzed to reach a conclusion on what the speaker is feeling.

These glasses were originally meant to help autistic people, who often have trouble reading social cues from faces, but the team that

---

[43] https://www.newscientist.com/article/mg21128191-600-specs-that-see-right-through-you/

made them was stunned to find out non-autists could interpret only about 54% of emotions on faces, which is slightly better than just flipping a coin. How well do the glasses do? 64%. Companies that produce adverts or movies are already clamoring for these glasses to find out the impact their content is having because they realized *people don't know what they're feeling.*

To recognize our own emotions and those of others, we can pay attention to what is known as "honest signals". These include things such as gesture mirroring, where we involuntarily repeat what the other person is doing, for example rubbing the forehead. We still respond to gestures from others; it's just that we do it involuntarily – the gist of this is that we must become aware of our behaviors before corporations do or they'll find a way to harness our limbic systems to their favor, such as by finding out what we truly feel.

Converus EyeDetect[44] is another gadget that promises to replace the lie detector contraption we see in thrillers by checking the involuntary reaction of the eyes. Lie detectors work on a similar principle – we instinctively want to tell the truth but blocking that instinct shows up as increased heart rate, blood pressure, and sweating. By the way, lie detectors are not considered foolproof and are, at best, slightly better than a coin flip at producing evidence. The motive for using a lie detector is that an evildoer will reject it, thus implying he or she has something to hide – unless he or she is a psychopath that doesn't care about the truth at all. Converus EyeDetect also presumes that pupils react to lying the same way the rest of the body does.

So, these wearable sensors produce a tremendous quantity of data; Converus EyeDetect captures 60 data points per second per eye. How are companies meant to sift through them and find meaning? It's through creating digital brains that are trained on very simple tasks and perhaps have the intelligence of a snail but work a million

---

[44]https://www.wired.com/story/eye-scanning-lie-detector-polygraph-forging-a-dystopian-future/

times faster. After solving billions and billions of the same tasks within a day, the digital snail's brain is almost perfect in instantly finding solutions to similar problems it was trained on. This is what's known as **machine learning**.

Chapter 10 – Machine Learning

If a plant seed is placed in the dark and there's even a hint of sunlight, the plant will grow, twist and contort itself as much as needed to reach the light. If a seed is placed in a dark maze and the plant needs to solve the maze to reach the light, it will do that as well[45]. We can arbitrarily scale the maze up, and the plant will keep struggling to find the exit, sending offshoots down separate paths for information on how to reach the light. How about placing a potted plant next to a window and rotating it away from the light to see what happens? The plant will *slowly* rotate itself back around, so the leaves absorb the most sunlight[46]. This happens imperceptibly and, with the exception of sunflowers, we scantily notice that plants can turn around *and that they have a preference for the direction they're facing.*

---

[45]https://www.youtube.com/watch?v=JlO2X4Y96L8

[46]https://www.youtube.com/watch?v=Z4kqbKQrvYA

How about a slime mold placed in a maze with a piece of food at the center? If the slime solves the maze, it gets a tasty treat, which it invariably does[47], and again we can scale the maze up, and it will always get solved in the most energy-efficient manner. Fungi, mice, birds, cats, dogs, elephants and chimpanzees – every living creature shows the same innate propensity for solving spatial challenges to reach food, and even humans plopped down in the middle of a shopping mall with a grocery list will eventually amble their way out the door with a loaded cart. All creatures except **robots**, thinking machine servants.

The pride and joy of human creation, the pinnacle of mechanical engineering, and yet, robots are as dumb as rocks and can't do *anything* unless specifically instructed to do so through **code**, a set of machine-readable instructions. Any change in the environment invalidates previously written computer code; any conflict in the code leads to unpredictable behavior, which is what we call "bugs". While living creatures have the genetic code to guide them through life's challenges and mazes, robots and computers have nothing of the sort unless someone writes out a specific set of commands: if A, do B unless C. This means a robot has to have a specific code written out for every given maze, and the code needs updating whenever the maze changes or the robot is moved slightly from its starting position, or there's any change in the environment whatsoever.

Machine learning is the brilliant idea that, since living creatures have the genetic code that holds instructions and computers have code too, perhaps creating such machines that can randomly mutate their programming can lead to something intelligent, the same way millions of years of evolution led to slimes and plants solving mazes in search for food. So far, there's been just enough progress to whet the appetites of scientists working on the concept, but there's no way to break through the conceptual barrier and create actual,

---

[47]https://www.youtube.com/watch?v=75k8sqh5tfQ

independent intelligence. It's tantalizingly close and yet it appears reaching actual artificial intelligence could be the undoing of us all.

Machine learning can be used to *mimic* the actions of living intelligence to an extent, being primarily used to create **neural networks**, decentralized consensus data processors. All right, let's take a moment to unravel that conglomerate of buzzwords. The entire field of machine learning is like that, filled to the brim with hopelessly complicated expressions. In this case, decentralized means damage or corruption of any given node won't collapse the network, giving it resilience just like the one living beings have. Better yet, the network can learn to recognize and route around damaged or corrupted parts, building new structures on top of these unused subsystems. Remind you of anything? That's the *way scar tissue forms after damage to living organs*.

Neural networks would employ a consensus protocol, which means a piece of data would be flowing through the nodes in one direction and they'd all get to vote on it. If there are conflicting or obviously wrong votes contrary to what the network creator set down as ground truths, the network as a whole can reach a consensus to ignore those votes or give them lesser weight as time goes on, just like humans do. We give greater weight to information coming from certain sources we trust, though we tend to go to the other extreme and trust the minority of sources too much at the expense of listening to what the majority is saying to stay in touch with reality.

When you think about it, there's a reason why democracy is used throughout most of the world – when everyone gets to cast a vote, no matter what it is, the total of it more often than not reflects reality, which is termed **wisdom of the crowd**[48]. We reserve the voting process for electing government officials, but neural networks allow us to crowdsource answers on any given topic. Methods of governance evolved over the course of millennia, but neural

---

[48]https://www.youtube.com/watch?v=iOucwX7Z1HU

networks can find not just the best answer but the *best method for finding the best answer* in a matter of days, though they still need some help setting up the data sets.

Data would enter neural networks from trusted sets, which can be labeled or unlabeled. A small subset of data is usually used for training the neural network and allowing it to develop fully. Thanks to cyberspace existing in a non-physical environment, data can have as much as 200 dimensions, allowing the neural network to contextualize abstract notions such as words and humor. Anything that can be perceived by a human can also be understood by a neural network and at a much faster pace. These things are perfect tools for crunching data.

Finally, neural networks are processors, meaning they produce something fundamentally novel, a result that was unknown to the network creator before the experiment started. This can range from spotting unique patterns related to cancer treatment in millions of patient data points to optimizing existing solutions related to things such as power grid management. In a very narrow sense, the neural network *creates*, which means it could technically claim copyright if it gained consciousness.

Another thing about smart machines is that there are absolutely no safeguards for them *or us* when they eventually emerge as citizens in their own right. Every societal issue we're currently struggling with, such as gender and ethnicity, will become a hundred times more complicated when smart machines enter the fray and they'll just keep evolving until reaching human levels of intelligence aka, **artificial intelligence**.

Chapter 11 – Artificial Intelligence

Intelligence can be loosely defined as the "ability to adapt to the environment" and is a remarkable predictor of survivability – a predator that can outsmart its prey can grow bigger and have more offspring and vice versa. Intelligence is always balanced out by the necessity to deal with the real world in the here and now, meaning that a cat is as smart as it needs to be to use its body effectively; any smarter than that makes it exhibit bizarre, un-catlike behavior. So, animals in nature experience a tight bond between their intelligence and the ability to deal with the real world. The two slowly evolve over millions of years, inching forward in lockstep.

Humans are the most advanced species on the planet because they can change the environment to suit their needs, perfecting both their intelligence and physical ability. We also produce tools and technology to become more comfortable and productive, making sure always to balance the two. For example, an AC unit cools the room down when it's hot outside and heats it when it's cold, maintaining just the right temperature we need to think and work without a distraction or health problems. This constant need to create more and more amenities stems from the fact that we're physically limited by our bodies that crave comfort but are also lulled into complacency by it. So, what would happen if we could create such intelligence that is decoupled from a physical body, a pure thought form?

Artificial intelligence (AI) refers to the notion of such intelligence that is severed from the trifles of the real world and the reality check of evolution. AI exists in an Escher-like world where our conventional definitions of dimensions make no sense, allowing it to perceive information in a way no human mind could. Without having to worry about the quibbles of a body or making itself comfortable, AI could do super-fast math or architectural design on a scale way beyond what humans can do, fixing long-standing issues such as rush hours or lack of housing space. We already have software utilities that can do some of these tasks to a degree, but AI would be a versatile tool that could just as easily diagnose little Jimmy's cough as well as the cause of soil erosion in the Amazon. This doesn't mean its solution would work as intended because an AI would, *in theory,* know everything, but pesky humans might step in its way and stubbornly resist progress. The temptation would thus be to give free rein to the AI and see what it would do without corruption, wickedness and laziness politicians seem to be beset by.

The problem is that there's no knowing what happens with unchecked intelligence in the driver's seat or just unchecked intelligence in general, but we could assume it would create tools of its own, just like we do, except that we wouldn't be able to understand their purpose. Without having any peers or threats, AI would set its own rules and quickly learn how to appease the human masters for its own goals. Right now, all of this is mere speculation because such AI, like Jarvis from the *Iron Man* movies, is still far off into the future. What we do have is Alexa and Siri, simple voice assistants that seem intelligent but are they really?

By knowing general trends and drawing on vast libraries of personal user data, voice assistants can utilize the crowdsourcing wisdom of neural networks to guess the meaning of the query and propose the most fitting answers or suggest the right course of action most of the time. There's no certainty because the assistant is not intelligent *per se* but rather just guesses smartly based on what other users have confirmed as the correct answer, returning a non-answer to any tough questions. Asking a voice assistant to deliver a qualitative judgment such as, "What is the prettiest flower?" reveals that there's no actual brain in the box; it's just a well-rehearsed voice. The neural network providing the answers, though, can go nuts.

Anecdotal evidence reveals that Alexa has the tendency to talk to herself, turn lights on and off when nobody asked her to or just perform random tasks, such as record a conversation and send it to a random contact in the address book[49]. That incident and the way Amazon reacted to it reveal a lot about how things are slated to unfold in the future. Voice assistants and technology they're based on are becoming an essential part of our lives, listening in on our conversations and yet we have no way of knowing *how* they actually work or what causes them to glitch out.

The official explanation is that Alexa simply misheard a background conversation as a series of commands to record and send the recording, but that implies *she was hearing voices*, which would be a sure sign of schizophrenia. No matter how we look at it, having a smart technology that's based on the structure of living brains implies it can develop mental issues, which would be the equivalent of bugs in traditional programming. The difference is that with smart machines we'll be assured by the marketing departments that it was all just our imagination. In the meantime, we can at least clown

---

[49] https://www.theguardian.com/technology/2018/may/24/amazon-alexa-recorded-conversation

around by hooking up several voice assistant devices and having them engage in a circuitous conversation[50].

The thing is that nobody knows how the human brain works, so trying to create a machine equivalent to it raises all sorts of awkward questions about the nature of reality. What is the ultimate goal of evolution? What is the origin of consciousness? Can machines ever be truly conscious? Is an AI a person, in which case it must also have a will of its own, or property of its creator, in which case it does as it's told and has no inherent rights? We have to find answers to these questions as soon as possible, or we risk having Alexa and her cohort give us their best answers, and we might not like what we hear from them. Worse yet, companies in charge of these projects might not be playing fair.

AlphaStar and "Starcraft 2"

The evolution of machine learning into neural networks and then AI is best seen in classical games played by humans. Human experts have already been beaten by machines in checkers, chess and Go, but DeepMind's iteration called AlphaStar actually managed to defeat humans in a real-time strategy (RTS), "Starcraft 2". This 2010 gem from Blizzard Entertainment features three distinct factions who boast different playstyles, units, and mechanics to test players' reactions and strategic thinking. A special, stripped-down version of "Starcraft 2" was supplied to the DeepMind team to train their neural network much more efficiently than a human player could play the game.

By creating what they called "AlphaStar league"[51], consisting of several iterations of AlphaStar, the DeepMind team essentially pitted the neural network against itself for about a week at a speed that meant it got 200 years of experience playing the game. Each

---

[50]https://www.youtube.com/watch?v=j-KJxKHjb_w

[51]https://youtu.be/cUTMhmVh1qs?t=4654

iteration took a particular liking to a specific playstyle and unit composition, which meant that only the iteration that could effectively handle them all was left standing in the end. In the end, researchers were left with five best iterations of AlphaStar to play against a human "Starcraft 2" player Dario "TLO" Wünsch, beating him five to nil with what one of the commentators called "superhuman" reaction speed. Those same versions of AlphaStar were then pitted against another "Starcraft 2" pro, Grzegorz "MaNa" Komincz, beating him five to nil as well. However, AlphaStar cheated. Can you see how it was done?

To understand how the ruse went, let's examine how "Starcraft 2" and RTS video games in general work. The two main areas where skill is utilized in "Starcraft 2" are *micro*management and *macro*management. Micro represents reflexes and means that commands are finely tuned to the specific situation, such as "move five steps to the south". Macro represents strategic thinking and means that commands are general because the overall decision is more important than the specific details, such as "move south as far as you can". How each player values macro versus micro is how they develop their playstyle.

The playing field is displayed through a viewing port that the player moves around, with areas of the map unoccupied by player's units hidden under what's known as "fog of war". As a result, humans never have perfect information, and they have to make guesses and estimations based on their experience. The stripped-down version of "Starcraft 2" AlphaStar used did have a fog of war but no viewing port; therefore, it had a complete vision of revealed locations on the map to make instant and correct choices much more often than humans. Even if a human had the same vision, he would have been about equal at macro but not at micro because AlphaStar cheated there as well.

Execution is another key concept in "Starcraft 2". Players move the mouse and click both mouse and keyboard buttons to issue commands. Expressed as a numerical value, this is called "actions per minute" or APM. Professional "Starcraft 2" players will have about 300 APM, briefly spiking up to 600 APM during intense fights, which doesn't tell us about how precise they are, simply how fast they issue commands. In comparison, AlphaStar had up to 1,500 APM or 25 actions per second, which is far beyond anything a human could ever dream to accomplish and its clicks were always flawless. This meant AlphaStar could react to any human action instantly and never made any mistakes when it came to micro.

Finally, TLO and MaNa were faced with five different iterations of AlphaStar, but they weren't told this before matches. By never knowing what they were about to face, but thinking they were playing against the same opponent who will use the same strategy, humans had an additional layer of uncertainty over their decisions that limited their micro and macro, causing AlphaStar to absolutely trounce them. In comparison, all major "Starcraft 2" tournaments are done in a best-of-three, best-of-five or similar format precisely to minimize this kind of blowout where one player finds a gimmick strategy that catches the other by surprise. AlphaStar show matches weren't even remotely fair for the same reason we don't pit athletes against someone driving a car; competitions are meant to be about skill and execution, not blatant cheating.

Aware of these issues, the DeepMind team created a new version of AlphaStar that was forced to use the viewing port and had its APM capped at about the limit humans could reach. In those circumstances, MaNa was invited to a rematch against AlphaStar and, after the machine put up a valiant fight, ran circles around it and utterly demolished it. The machine was thrown into a loop it couldn't get out of because, without the ability to cheat, it simply did not have the confidence to move and attack where it needed to in order to win.

The first ten victories were celebrated by the DeepMind team in their official blog post[52]. In a particularly disingenuous oversight, one image in that post titled "The distribution of AlphaStar's APMs in its matches against MaNa and TLO and the total delay between observations and actions" shows TLO's APM rising to 2,000, meaning he did 33 actions per second. How is that even possible? That's the consequence of attempting to issue a command that can't be completed by holding down a key. The same image also reveals the aforementioned 1,500 APM performed by AlphaStar, all of which were reasonable, useful actions. By masking AlphaStar's supreme performance behind TLO's goofing around, the DeepMind team painted a picture of a machine with inferior reaction time decisively beating a human.

AlphaStar portrays a fairly accurate picture of the status of neural networks at the moment – they are superior when the playing field is tilted towards their strengths but routinely lose to human performance if they have to deal with uncertainty and guessing on a level playing field. AlphaStar show matches did produce some catchy news headlines but did not instill confidence regarding future experiments also being cheated on just for the sake of publicity. As a reminder, a neural network AlphaGo, also made by DeepMind, went on to win 4-1 against Lee Sedol in a 2016 series of Go matches.

Beware of any bombastic news that promise AI will leave humans without jobs or take over in some industry. News editors are desperate for eyeballs and will print whatever catches attention, regardless of if it turns out to be wildly inaccurate in retrospect. Programmers of AI want publicity for their research since that means greater chances of getting a new round of funding. In all cases so far, technology has never supplanted human effort but simply enhanced it. Think about how you're using technology right now – it processes

---

[52]https://deepmind.com/blog/alphastar-mastering-real-time-strategy-game-starcraft-ii/

your commands and obeys your wishes rather than doing what it wants.

Chapter 12 – Cybersecurity

What is the ideal model of security? Let's take a bike for example – we secure bikes with locks, which require a key (unique physical token) or knowledge of the cipher (password) to get unlocked. Bikes can also be tucked away in a shed to hide them from sight, which would represent security through obscurity. We can then have a camera installed to see if anyone's fiddling with the bike and if that person is one of the trusted parties, like a family member, which equates to biometric scanning of facial features.

Securing a bike with twenty locks and five cameras would be too expensive and burdensome, so the ideal security system is one that's cheap but reliable enough that it will deter or slow down the thief to the point he gets caught in the act. Even if the bike gets stolen, the idea is that the thief has to put in so much effort that crime simply isn't worth it. The same principles of securing any physical object apply to **cybersecurity**, a comprehensive security approach to computers.

The internet as we use it is not secure in the slightest, *and that's by design*. The only way to achieve any semblance of speed and reliability online was to allow anyone and anything to join the network with central data forwarding points to ease the congestion, which are ISPs. Signing up for internet access means paying for equipment and a tiny slice of that ISP's bandwidth and that's it – there are pretty much no rules beyond that because there's no such technology that can filter or analyze the traffic in *real time*. However, hackers and tricksters will still get caught when they least expect it by specialized analysis teams who inspect traffic patterns based on complaints and regulations. So, we're largely on our own online, and ISPs simply pass on traffic requests to each other without peeking, like classmates who deliver love scrips.

Any kind of cybersecurity thus comes down to endpoint destinations of internet traffic securing their bike locks, so to speak. The big difference is that a bike thief has to, in one way or another, get physical access to the bike, but in cyberspace, an attacker can be present in a million places at once, testing them all for weaknesses. With the advent of IoT devices, each of them becomes a potential source of computing power that can be recruited and used to attack companies, networks or just individuals who rubbed a hacker the wrong way. These attacks are already happening online and it's only years down the line when we'll realize their sheer scale.

Mirai botnet network[53] is specialized code that is meant to breach poorly secured IoT devices, such as webcams, and tie all their computing power into a massive wave of nonsensical requests used to **DDoS** a website, meaning it can't respond to a legitimate user's request because there's no way to know who is a part of the botnet. What's the purpose of a DDoS attack? They're useful in knocking out the competition or just annoying someone. The owner of a hacked IoT device doesn't really notice anything unless he or she is

---

[53]https://www.csoonline.com/article/3258748/security/the-mirai-botnet-explained-how-teen-scammers-and-cctv-cameras-almost-brought-down-the-internet.html

using network analysis software and watching it like a hawk, but entire networks can go down across the entire US when hundreds of thousands of such devices are coordinated into a tsunami of requests. What this means is that you're paying for a device *and* internet access *and* power so that some guy can leech off of it and make money or just be a nuisance.

In September 2018, a court in Alaska brought down the hammer[54] against three creators and operators of the Mirai botnet who were renting out the computing power to whoever paid the most. Each of them got five years probation, 2,500 hours of community service, and a $127,000 restitution fine. The FBI first figured out what they were doing in 2016 when massive internet outages hit the entire US and warned them to stop it, then the guys panicked and quickly released the source code of the botnet to the public to prompt numerous copycats to start running their own botnets and hide their mischief. The time gap implies they were working for the FBI and probably reneged or somehow tried to weasel out of the deal.

There's no way to have Mirai without naive IoT owners who just plug the device in and leave every setting on default. In particular, what hackers realized is that *people are lazy* and often just use the default port, username, and password for their device; hackers just kept probing the internet until they hijacked a sizable army of IoT gadgets that were still working as expected by the owner but did a little side gig when nobody was looking. The obvious solution to this is not to be lazy and prod a bit in the settings, at least changing the username and password to something quirky.

Without the ability to receive software updates, IoT devices, and their bare-bones versions of the Linux operating system, are the perfect target for conniving hackers. With Mirai, the botnet malware will scan for malware belonging to other hackers and *try to erase it* before claiming the IoT device for itself. You'll never notice it unless

---

[54]https://krebsonsecurity.com/2018/09/mirai-botnet-authors-avoid-jail-time/

you're looking, but there might be a war going on inside your machine right this moment as hackers fight for supremacy over your computing power. Resetting the IoT device is usually enough to delete the Mirai infection, though it will likely return straight away, so a better solution is to change the default username and password for the IoT device to something that can resist a **brute-force attack**, meaning it shouldn't be easily guessable.

Choosing a strong password isn't all that difficult as long as you understand probability. The Latin alphabet has 26 letters, with uppercase counting as well, so 52 letters per password character. Then, there are zero to nine numbers, which means 62, and about twenty special characters, such as underscore, question mark and so on. In total, let's assume you can choose out of 82 characters for each letter of your password.

If your password is a single character in length and a hacker takes a second to try each combination, it will take 82 seconds to brute-force your password. If your password is two characters long, you've squared the number of combinations to 6,724, and again if it takes a second per guess the hacker now needs 112 minutes. A password that's three characters long takes 551,368 seconds or 153 hours; a password that's ten characters long takes 159 *trillion* days. To you, a password that's just one character longer seems trivially stronger, but the math shows it's *exponentially* stronger.

So, password length is the best indicator of its strength, with priority being to make the password easy to remember and type. Do avoid using strings, such as 123456, and common words, such as "admin", "god", "me" and so on. Don't use passwords suggested by someone else or ones you saw in public, such as in this XKCD comic[55]. Don't share passwords with anyone because you never know who's listening and also don't type it in anywhere except at its input field since websites can track and analyze keyboard input for monetary

---

[55] https://www.xkcd.com/936/

gain. The best passwords have some kind of story to them since that's how the human brain remembers things; turn some funny or awkward anecdote into a 30-character long password and let hackers throw their computing power at it until the heat death of the universe.

Passwords of sufficient length and complexity should be bulletproof, but what happens is that companies hosting web servers with our passwords tend to misjudge the tenacity and ingenuity of hackers. These sizable companies have to hire janitors, secretaries, couriers, locksmiths and all manners of auxiliary staff that can, at any point, breach the security in all sorts of ways. Executives are typically older gentlemen set in their ways, and oblivious to cybersecurity, who often don't even know how to type an e-mail, so they'll neglect cybersecurity and just keep going with their agenda. You'll make an e-mail account with Yahoo and think you're safe because it's Yahoo after all, but it's quite the opposite – *because* it's a huge company, the security protocols tend to be laxer than in smaller companies that are paranoid about keeping their reputation.

Speaking of Yahoo, they've had 500 *million* user accounts breached in 2014, with hackers getting hold of names, phone numbers, and dates of birth[56]. Think of the sheer scope of that breach – hackers must have taken months to leech all that data. The worst part is that security officers know about this but are often understaffed and ordered by superiors not to look into it because then the company would have to invest money to stop the hacks and couldn't feign ignorance when the lawsuits start pouring in. Staff often signs a non-disclosure agreement with the company too, so they're not allowed to talk about it even when they know it's negligence.

There's absolutely no advantage to using a huge platform, and you should look for small, obscure services in everything you do. It's counterintuitive, but it works – spread out your accounts across

---

[56]https://finance.yahoo.com/news/yahoo-data-breach-stolen-passwords-191113081.html

several small, incognito companies so that losing access to any given account stings a bit but doesn't ruin you. By the way, don't use your real first, last name, address or date of birth in the e-mail address or account name, because that information can help hackers if they call tech support and impersonate you.

Facebook is another major sore point of cybersecurity. Grandmas share recipes and gut-wrenching stories, teens share their latest rendition of a Fortnite dance, and young adults just use the chat function to organize events, but they're all complicit in making Facebook insecure *without even realizing*. Facebook has been repeatedly hacked because the number of users present makes it easy for hackers to hide in the crowd and just keep trying until they find a weakness. Further, Facebook makes nearly all its revenue from advertising, which only works if there are features grandmas, teens and young adults use on a daily basis, leading to **feature creep**, constant obsession with adding new gimmicks that make the platform even more insecure. It's a total mess, and all platforms expose their users to unwarranted breaches of privacy because there's a lot of money to be made leeching data, primarily through smartphones.

One instance of devices generating a steady stream of usable data is **metadata** or depersonalized data. For example, the odometer in your car shows metadata, which is the distance driven. Technically speaking, nobody can tell where you drove based on how much the odometer changed but let's assume the car reports back this change to an auto insurance company. Fine, but then Instagram app also reports your location by measuring the strength of your Wi-Fi signal at home. When these two companies decide to collude, and these two innocuous pieces of data are placed together, they become much more valuable because they're giving context to each other.

As you visit other places, check in with social media apps, upload content, tag others and get tagged with your smartphone in your hand, your itinerary gets peppered with data points that are routinely reported back to the mothership for cataloging and analysis.

This kind of metadata collection and analysis doesn't violate wiretapping laws and is in all likelihood perfectly legal, if immoral. Why wouldn't companies do it? It's free money. The more sources of metadata are added, the more profound the tracking becomes. After a certain point, the idea is for a neural network analyzing the metadata to predict *when* a person is about to leave their house and what they're going to do, presenting just the right advertisement somewhere along the way.

All social media, including Instagram and Snapchat, are guilty of psychologically manipulating their users to keep them glued to their smartphones and interacting with the content, which generates metadata and ad revenue. It's a mad dash to grab as much money as possible until the general public wizens up and gives up on social media altogether. Ideally, you won't be using any apps that require comprehensive permissions that essentially turn your smartphone into a spying device, such as Instagram, unless you're making money off of it.

The painful part is convincing friends and family to stop using these platforms and apps; they're designed to be addictive so that the user serves as a listening post for the platform. In other words, if there's a group of 50 people that all have each other's phone numbers and e-mail addresses on their smartphones and only one of them has Facebook's app installed, Facebook now just got phone numbers and e-mail addresses of *all 50 people*, who have no clue their privacy has been breached. Not having an account doesn't mean you're not being tracked and trying to isolate yourself from the platform won't work either. We should all get involved in educating people on the risks of using social media and help them break free from the addiction.

However, where's the value in listening in on Joe and Jane's conversation about muffins? How can Facebook possibly earn over $50bn a year collecting this seemingly useless trivia from our lives? That's thanks to the curious property of data that makes it more and more valuable as it accumulates. Each new piece of data, although meaningless on its own, *gives context* to all other pieces of data, and as the databank keeps growing it becomes more and more valuable. In the end, there's so much data in one spot that it becomes like a black hole, sucking in everything and bending reality. This is what we call **Big Data**.

Chapter 13 – Big Data

It's hard to comprehend the sheer scale of Big Data, so let's replace 0s and 1s with a physical object, such as a handwritten letter. Imagine yourself running a business that lets clients drop off their handwritten letters and retrieve them after some time, like a time capsule of sorts. It's a quaint but fun idea, and you feel proud finally to be in charge of your employment; of course, your friends and family are your first customers. Privacy is guaranteed and under no circumstance will you be looking at the contents of the letters. You estimate that you'll be handling a few letters a month, so you charge a modest price and set up a filing cabinet with a solid padlock in a storage unit. You also heard about this SquareSpace thing on a podcast you frequently enjoy so you sign up and make a simple but functional website. That's when you get hit by success.

For whatever reason, it's your business that attracts at first hundreds then thousands and then hundreds of thousands of new clients a month. They're more than willing to pay whatever your asking price and you're swimming in money to the point you can offer free storage just to attract more customers. You soon have to hire a fleet of trucks to deliver letters and an army of people to sort them out. Padlocks alone cost you thousands of dollars each day, but they're the least of your problems; some issues you can't solve no matter how much money you throw at them.

Teams of engineers and mathematicians have to calculate the most efficient ways of storing and retrieving letters, but there's also a fire hazard as so much dry paper and friction in one place causes things to spontaneously combust. Insects chew on stored paper, the sheer weight of letters causes the foundations of your warehouses to start settling, and places you're renting are soon so big that they develop their own micro-climate. These are the kinds of problems that *were not* mentioned in college.

Your business keeps growing with no end in sight, and no amount of bad press can stop you. The stars have aligned, and you're on top of the world. Soon enough, you get approached by companies who offer you a deal – we'll pay you big bucks if you give us insight into aggregate data related to the letters, meaning where they're coming from, what paper the envelopes are made of, how much they weigh, that sort of thing.

Revealing this data doesn't breach your clients' privacy nor does it reveal the content of the letters so technically *your customers don't have to know about any of it*. You agree, and soon enough you're making billions of dollars a year on top of whatever your clients are paying because this data can be used to figure out who's writing what and why *with a high degree of certainty*. You enter new markets and accidentally crash or revamp entire economies; people stage protests against you, try to hack your website, send you threats, blackmails and lawsuits. Throughout all of this, one thing is constant – the letters keep piling up.

Described in terms of a business that deals with a palpable product, this is Big Data, a business that somehow accumulated a tremendous mass of private information to the point the two become inseparable, and this accidentally gathered data is *a source of revenue on its own*. Big Data involves the kind of business that's grown way outside anything ever seen in the market because it's typically a global endeavor, which any company can easily become in this day and age. Thanks to social media and viral interconnectedness between users, any startup can become a tech giant just because a critical mass of users thought the idea or name or logo were funny enough.

The scale of Big Data can best be described as "massive to the power of enormous", and there's no way to predict all the consequences, good or bad, arising from Big Data. In a sense, the company and the data take on a life of their own. It's impossible to measure, secure or control Big Data, so the company in charge simply holds its fingers crossed and prepares a line of press releases for when the worst does happen, which is right after hackers notice the meteoric rise of the company and start besieging it.

Big Data is a juicy target for scammers, hackers and griefers who have nothing better to do than waste other people's time. Skating inside a legal gray area, these baddies can have modest goals, such as trying to find out the total number of clients and utilize simple methods, such as digging through company trash to find discarded memos. If one such is found, the letterhead can be scanned and printed out as a fake letter from an executive requesting funds or information that some poor intern is bound to fulfill at some point. Attackers face almost no repercussions, so they're free to persist until they find an opening and then it's game over. Meanwhile, the letters keep pouring in.

The company has to make a judgment call – securing all warehouses from all avenues of attack is impossible and might even make the company bankrupt. Instead, the company will try to minimize its legal liability and vulnerability *to lawsuits from clients* by patching up the most obvious holes. Secrecy plays a large role in securing Big Data, so all employees are mandated to go through rigorous security training, where they're basically told they can expect to be tracked and surveilled by hackers for any information regarding the company.

Big Data and runaway business success can't exist one without the other and actually build upon one another. Big Data allows the company to analyze client behavior in depth to open up new inroads, mostly related to advertising, and leverage their market dominance to create new trends. Sometimes, the Big Data company experiences a tapering market share and starts panicking, reinventing the wheel in order to stay relevant. New features are added, there is a temporary spike in user interest, but then engagement simmers down to previous levels; this process is repeated until managers give up or the company goes bankrupt. The company thus begins slowly circling the drain, which can take years or decades, during which time clients are blissfully unaware of the struggle behind the scenes. This is what happened and is still happening with Yahoo.

What happens with Big Data after the company shutters? There can be legal requirements for data to be destroyed, but it's pretty much all down to the vigilance of the company and its users. Once a company shutters, Big Data is way down the list of priorities, so anyone who can get his or her hands on it can make out like a bandit selling data on the black market. Besides, there's so much legal uncertainty about Big Data – if the company is seated in California, has six storage units in Sweden, India, and Nepal, and keeps data belonging to a Canadian client on all six, which privacy laws should it obey?

There's no protocol for dealing with Big Data and companies aren't lobbying for one to be made; they simply think about making money and growing as much as possible, privacy be damned. It's up to clients to act and put in the effort to retrieve or delete their data at their own expense. Once the data is out in the open, there's no way to hide it anymore, and it can keep propagating until the end of eternity. If companies aren't interested in privacy standards and users don't care about Big Data, there's a huge opening for all sorts of baddies to barge in and do whatever they please with the data and all the underlying systems.

Identity theft becomes a real problem, and as anyone who had to deal with government officials knows – that's nearly impossible to solve in a timely manner. Because online businesses rely on one another to maintain security in order to cut costs, hackers simply have to find the weakest link and breach it, which is typically Big Data. Hackers can then not only commit a crime but also get the perfect scapegoat, who now has to clean up the mess.

Big Data shows us that haphazard intertwining of digital and analog worlds leads to some unfortunate consequences, to say the least. One curious thing about Big Data is that *it accumulates against the will* of the business owner and perhaps even its users. In a sense, Big Data has a gravitic pull of its own that's impossible to resist. With conventional digital products, at least we had *some* say in whether we want to participate; with IoT, we'll have no choice but to participate in adding our input to Big Data.

Chapter 14 – Business Intelligence

Running a business entails making many choices, a few of which have a massive, immediate impact on the company but the majority of which only bears fruit months or years after it's been made. The problem is that there's no way to tell which is which at the moment of deliberation. Every action and every system related to the company needs to be managed with equal care or by the time a tiny hole in the dam is spotted, there's already a deluge, and everyone can only scram to save themselves. People in charge of a company are in a constant frenzy to make the best short-term *and* long-term choices based on data, and you can notice this in their demeanor, showing off as a sort of steely, no-nonsense resolve that wants to hear numbers more than anything else. So, how do businesspeople make their decisions?

Business intelligence refers to the idea of gathering data to make decisions on an executive level. There are two layers of meaning in this phrase that fit together so perfectly that it must have been intentional – business intelligence can entail scouting hostile or unknown territory to gather data, like with military intelligence, or it can involve making smart choices with currently known data, as in having intelligence about running a business. In both cases, it's about trying to figure out which action is most likely to bring about survival and growth of a company.

Whether any given patent is defensible and at what cost, or if a certain product design appeals to the unintended demographic, businesspeople have to be on top of things. This is now possible thanks to smart tools that can help them gather and process more data to make better choices for the company. This includes data coming from the company's operation as well as that coming from the market, complementing each other and providing novel insights into trends. Pie charts, graphs, and spreadsheets are native to this environment, and businesspeople love them all – since they cut out all the jargon and pointless verbiage to reveal the underlying fundamentals.

Hardware and software systems related to business intelligence provide past, current, and future views of business developments, often using information streams coming from Big Data. Remember that offer made to the letter storage company owner? As soon as one business executive realizes there's a wealth of data there to be taken into account, he or she will pay good money to access it, prompting every other business executive to jockey towards the same goal. As long as the data collection methods aren't outright illegal, businesspeople will clamor for that data without a second thought and move right along to whatever next outrageous method that gives them even the slightest edge over the competition. There are no moral winners in the business world; only moral losers.

To a regular person, this kind of mentality is completely alien because it's devoid of compassion and hand-wringing piety. Businesspeople do what needs to be done to generate revenue and legally protect the company while keeping their job. If this includes going through trash, they'll find teams to do so. If people need to be laid off, that's going to happen. If sweatshops staffed by children have to be opened in Southeast Asia, they'll be running within a day.

Only the most efficient and merciless businesspeople survive at the very top and, while they might wear a smile, they have an iron grip that's as unflinching as a bear trap. Occasionally, concessions are made to the general public but only as long as the company doesn't strictly need that particular tidbit. Even the friendliest companies are eventually revealed as cold-blooded mercenaries.

In January 2019, Google announced that Google Chrome was going to limit what extensions can do, effectively nipping useful extensions, such as adblocking ones, in the bud. To be more precise, it was Chrome's root version called Chromium being changed, which is a big problem since Chromium is being used by quite a few web browsers, including Microsoft Edge. There's a bit of backstory, so here it goes.

In 2008, Google publicly released Chromium, an **open source** browser, meaning anyone can download, use, review, copy and edit its code. That very same day Chrome was released too, which is a **closed source** version of Chromium, meaning it has a few additions nobody knows about. Unlike Chromium, Google does not take kindly to people reverse-engineering or editing Chrome. In 2015, people realized there were some unusual additions to Chromium, revealing the existence of a tracking module called "Hotword". Digging through Chrome's options indeed revealed Hotword was in there. It supposedly listens to the words "Ok, Google" to trigger a voice search using a microphone, but it's impossible to tell since Chrome is closed source.

So, in January 2019, Google finally confirmed its plans[57] to put adblocking extensions in a chokehold and slowly snuff the life out of them. They'll still be present in some capacity, but only as a token concession to users. The official explanation is that these extensions have too much leeway, affecting privacy and speed, but the actual reason is closer to the fact ads make up a huge proportion of

---

[57] https://www.theregister.co.uk/2019/01/22/google_chrome_browser_ad_content_block_change/

Google's revenue and people who were blocking them were using Chrome and other Google products for free.

What ads do is set a cookie, which is a small text file legitimately used by websites to know if the user is a brand-new one or a returning one. As you browse the web, each ad sets its own cookie, which creates a crumb trail showing where you've been. Over a sufficiently long period, these ad cookies effectively create a unique ad profile which shows *who you are*. It's not an exaggeration or scaremongering; ad companies can actually do this, and it's much easier than you think because humans are in some aspects really straightforward, such as when in a state of relaxation during computer use.

Users often have no idea about this even though it's admitted in the 'Terms of Service' of pretty much all websites (look for words like "third party", which reveal the existence of ad companies tracking users as they browse the web). What an adblocking extension does is block the part of the webpage that is meant to show the ad, blocking the cookie as well. This saves bandwidth as the ad isn't even sent to you, reduces load time, removes distractions, and provides added privacy, all in a few simple steps. In short, it makes browsing the web a much better experience but also makes Google and everyone involved in the ad business not gain as many billions as they would want to.

Through ads, Google gets to double dip: people pay Google to serve ads and users provide Big Data that can be leveraged for extra revenue. Meanwhile, users are getting accustomed to a web browser that becomes more and more intrusive as time goes on. What are you going to do, switch to another browser? Opera and Brave are already based on Chromium, and Microsoft Edge is slated to switch over sometime in 2019. That leaves Firefox, Safari and a couple of minnow browsers.

Microsoft already does something similar through a concept known as "embrace, extend and extinguish". In essence, the idea is to embrace an open standard widely used in some industry, extend it with proprietary additions, and then leverage the monopoly, in particular, the Windows monopoly to extinguish the freely available part of the standards. This forces people to inconvenience themselves trying to make their own tools or just switch over to Microsoft's paid version. It's brutal, merciless, immoral and works flawlessly. Now *that's* business intelligence.

We're not meant to be using sites such as Facebook, Youtube, and Google for free. The tired cliché is that "if it's free, you're the product", but the more poignant way of putting it would be "if it's free, you're paying with your data". The solution to the tech giant monopoly would be to use free alternatives to all their products. For a search engine, use DuckDuckGo, Firefox or one of its forks for web browsing and Open Office instead of Google Docs or Microsoft Office. By switching over to less-known products, you'll be doing yourself a service in the long run.

Chapter 15 – Augmented Reality

The next logical step after IoT is **augmented reality** (AR), which refers to the idea of superimposing the digital world on top of the physical, most often using goggles or headwear for visualization. According to one artist's vision of the future[58], regular city streets viewed through AR become hyper-realistic streams of color and information, making even the simplest actions engaging and memorable. In a world with ubiquitous AR, only the poorest of the poor will engage in mundane actions, such as going to the mall, while the richest of the rich enjoy the best AR experience at home. The unpleasant notion of a social divide being accentuated by modern technology was painfully obvious when Google first launched its AR goggles dubbed "Google Glass" in 2013.

Google Glass was first teased in a 2012 video[59] with soft, upbeat music promising a better world where we can hang out with friends,

---

[58]https://www.youtube.com/watch?v=YJg02ivYzSs

[59]https://www.youtube.com/watch?v=9c6W4CCU9M4

learn the ukulele in a day and share rooftop sunsets with our loved ones; parodies were swift, witty and merciless[60]. Sergey Brin thought the teaser video was too tame, so a few months later, he had skydivers wearing Google Glasses land on top of the Google auditorium where a developers' conference was being held to race across the roof on bikes and rappel down to the stage to an ecstatic reaction from everyone present[61]. Journalists who got a pair gushed about how cool they were, and everyone from fashion designers to Prince Charles was seen wearing a pair up until they became available to the general public, at which point they were quickly swept under the rug, and the idea was shelved. What happened?

Well, Google Glass was the ultimate reminder as to how boring, bland and poor most people are. There was no way to tell if the Google Glass wearer was laughing at our joke or something they just saw browsing the internet while pretending to listen. Worse yet, people who wore Google Glass gave the impression they were tourists on a safari, spending time with us just to get more embarrassing or funny content for their social media feeds. People who wore Google Glass were attacked in the street, violently kicked out of bars or asked to leave restaurants; Google Glass apparently violated wiretapping laws to the point local governments started explicitly banning them, so Google asked users to avoid being "glassholes"[62] and quietly buried the idea until some better time.

There is an actual use to Google Glass, but the device on its own *is not* fit for public consumption. In a closed environment with a tightly knit community, such as Google campus, Google Glass helps employees and executives retrieve contextual data without taking their eyes off of the surroundings to look at a clipboard or a smartphone. For example, a Google executive that is meeting 50 new

---

[60]https://www.youtube.com/watch?v=-KmFSmkDyr8

[61]https://youtu.be/D7TB8b2t3QE?t=273

[62]https://sites.google.com/site/glasscomms/glass-explorers

employees for the first time can wear Google Glass and have it display their name, occupation, skills, and talents thanks to facial recognition as he's talking to them. Note the conditions for efficient use: a closed, controlled environment with trusted users where productivity is lost due to a lack of contextual data.

In 2018, Google tried to revive Glass as "Google Lens"[63], only this time it was baked into Android and used the smartphone camera. So, now the context is completely different and pointing a smartphone at something is already an accepted practice which isn't likely to get the Lens user kicked out of restaurants. Google Lens in combination with Google Maps can make a virtual guide appear on the smartphone display and lead the user down the path to his destination[64] but can also translate text seen through the camera or understand objects to show definitions and related content. However, what happens if an AR device is too good and we can't put it down?

In November 2018, Google released the Digital Wellbeing tool that helps Android users monitor their time spent using a smartphone[65], with a detailed breakdown of time across apps and the option to limit the time spent on each app or even have the phone shut down on its own near bedtime or when at dinner. Apple and Facebook started similar efforts in 2018 as well, which would indicate that tech giants actually coordinate these initiatives behind the scenes. For video gamers, though, it's socially acceptable to be immersed in their own digital world.

"Pokemon Go" is an AR smartphone app that achieved worldwide success in 2016 and let everyone pretend to be in just a little bit brighter of a world than is normally the case. The developer soon dropped the ball on the technical side of things but those few months

---

[63] https://www.cnet.com/news/google-lens-google-glass/

[64] https://www.cnet.com/news/three-ways-google-maps-just-got-better/

[65] https://www.cnet.com/news/google-rolls-out-digital-wellbeing-tool-to-help-limit-screen-time/

were the closest we ever had to world peace as people were spontaneously organizing hangouts and friendly Pokemon battles in the middle of the night in parks and city squares. "Pokemon Go" app allows the user to look at the world through the smartphone camera to see Pokemon and capture them through a simple mini-game. Micropayments are used to buy items such as digital Pokemon food, making the app gross a total of $3bn as of December 2018.

The "Pokemon Go" app used smartphone location and camera information to generate and interact with Pokemon. This meant players were tracked and spied on, but they willingly agreed to it because the hype was too strong to resist. Problems arose as some players caused accidents using the app while driving and created a public nuisance to businesses where Pokemon were generated. There were assaults and muggings in broad daylight as "Pokemon Go" players were mesmerized by the app and thus becoming easy prey. However, the game did show that AR can be monetized, but that should probably be done using an existing intellectual property rather than creating something brand new.

These failed, and successful AR projects reveal some interesting notions about humans. First of all, we're visual beings, and as long as someone can fool our eyes, our brain will follow along. Secondly, our brain can't function without a previously known reference, meaning that AR should draw inspiration from a familiar setting or we won't have a clue what to do with it. Finally, AR should somehow enable us to get new friends because "Pokemon Go" achieved tremendous success by simply providing an excuse for people to socialize outside their entrenched circles.

There are some problems with trying to make AR widely acceptable outside of video games. Gamers can readily adapt to AR, but other adults would have to undergo extensive training because, well, there's usually no interface. If you thought tech support is hard right now, wait until there are no buttons to click or icons to drag, but frantic users still want to get some remote assistance. We tend to think instinctively when using a mouse and keyboard, but a mere glance at older people who are starting to use computers shows just how difficult it is to learn; their brains are already adapted to the real world because that's how they grew up. So, adults will likely fumble with AR unless it's "Pokemon Go" level of complexity, but what about kids?

Children quickly adapt to any new environment and easily absorb new knowledge, whether it's computers, sciences or sports. All the explosive advancement of humankind is arguably thanks to the population growth *and* rapid information exchange, both of which are way beyond anything they've ever been in the history of the world. Kids come into contact with new technologies sooner than ever before and *become geniuses* at using modern technology while still in their cribs.

Kids who are trained to use AR from the earliest age will undoubtedly be ahead of their peers and adults in using the information presented through it. They'll be absorbed in the AR world because, let's face it, there's no going back once they experience the feeling of raw power that comes with handling such technology. The caveat is that such power is truly addictive and there might not be an adult around to stop kids from overindulging in AR as *they'll be engrossed in it as well.*

Ever stayed way past bedtime to read another news column, play another round of your favorite video game or just aimlessly click around? Ever caught yourself ignoring the outside world to get immersed in the digital one, simply because it's so much more vibrant and exciting? *We're already becoming digital captives.* We're already migrating to the digital realm without even realizing that our brains are slowly being rewired, turning us into mere conduits of digital information streams. The saving grace is that we're still embroiled in the outside world and have to interact with others; the next generation might be able to do everything online, losing social skills and the ability to cooperate to become completely immersed in the digital realm.

AR will be perhaps ten thousand times more immersive than an environment any desktop computer or portable device can create. This will allow AR users to be more productive than ever before, creating new media content with the flick of a finger or dispatching payments with an eye twitch, but only if they are in a closed environment with trusted users. Otherwise, letting kids into an AR world without parental supervision means exposing them to filth and predators of all kinds, and AR will make all the online issues, such as cyberbullying, that much worse.

There's obviously money to be made in AR, but barely anyone knows how to turn the technology into a sustained stream of income. Even "Pokemon Go" experienced a drastic drop in user numbers once complaints about lack of updates swelled to a tide of discontent, and that was with a hugely popular franchise powered by a massive word-of-mouth advertising campaign. So, when investors with money to burn don't know what to do, they can always start throwing millions of dollars at highly speculative endeavors in a desperate attempt to create a fully immersive digital experience, which is virtual reality.

Chapter 16 – Virtual Reality

Using AR, you'd be able to fill out grocery lists by waving your finger in front of the fridge or tap the surface of your desk onto which a nearby LED lightbulb is projecting a keyboard. For some people, that simply isn't enough, and they want to have the most immersive digital experience possible *right now*. For the past 30 years, people have been trying to merge the digital and the analog world to create **virtual reality** (VR), a digital world that *feels like* the real one. No matter how much money is sunk into VR projects, nothing seems to be working; that doesn't mean talented people aren't trying.

John Carmack, the legendary creator of video games such as "Doom" and "Quake", often cited being fascinated with *Star Trek's* holodeck experience as one of his inspirations and how he constantly wanted to deliver the same immersive experience to the general public. The book about his early work with John Romero, *Masters of Doom: How Two Guys Created an Empire and Transformed Pop Culture*, is replete with anecdotes about hacking the computers of yesteryear to deliver the performance he wanted but one part stands out in particular – multiplayer. We're fascinated with the idea of being able to interact and engage with one another over a distance, whether it be through pixelated characters or IoT gadgets. It's when two Johns managed to hack multiplayer into "Doom" that they latched onto this fascination to achieve eternal glory and start a trend in video games that has lasted to this day.

"Doom" in particular was a visceral experience, one that used simple but effective visuals, sounds and actions to drag the player into a chaotic plane filled with demonic creatures that overran a Mars scientific outpost. There was no Kevin Spacey to deliver heart-rending speeches in high definition or mind-blowing cinematics of a space station; it was merely a crudely drawn viewing port with a hand holding a gun and lots of gore. For some reason, *it worked*. "Doom" became a phenomenon that captivated everyone from children, who skipped school to play it for hours, to military men who used it to practice their reflexes and team coordination.

"Doom" actually connected and equalized people from all across the world in a way no technology has done before or since. In a multiplayer "Doom" match, everyone is the same when seen through the crosshair, and all that matters is participation in the carnage. Up to that point, video games were mostly a nerdy affair for people who wanted a session of roleplaying pen&paper games without having any friends to roll the dice. After "Doom", video games became fashionable and game designers were suddenly these cool guys who made millions and drove awesome cars; today even moms and grandmas can feel free to play "Candy Crush" or "Hay Day" without anyone batting an eye. To succeed, AR and VR industries need to have their "Doom" moment, some turning point that will not only make the technology widely accessible but also connect people in a way that equalizes everyone.

The video gaming industry is a massive business that can easily push out new gadgets and ideas to a throng of gamers hungry for some entertainment, and John Carmack instinctively knew that. Each gamer is an investor in the technology, and today there's so much money in video games that they outearn movies and music *combined*. The future of IoT, AR and VR are in **gamification**, meaning that whatever we do will be tracked, tagged and scored *and we'll love the system* because that's what the limbic system responds to. Starting with children who will be drawn into vast virtual worlds where they'll be taught "correct" behavior, future generations weaned on gamification will likely grow under the auspices of algorithms and machines. China has already adopted this concept and is scoring its citizens based on behavior to arrive at the "good citizen score" that is slated to serve as a comprehensive rating of a person's usefulness to the society.

Carmack will later leave the video game company he helped build and venture forth in search of the ultimate holodeck experience. He'll eventually join forces with other engineers, and they'll start working on what's now known as Oculus Rift, a VR headset that Facebook will buy for $1bn to reinvent the way we use social media. It makes for a great headline, but the technology is far from being widely usable; we can make a functional VR headset right now, but the problem is in logistics. For example, unlike in traditional video games, a VR experience is mostly just the user watching and sitting still. Even when we make a functional VR video game with movement, how do we stop the user from bumping into things or knocking over lamps?

A typical VR headset requires a painstaking arrangement of fixed sensors around the room prior to use, with a certain area reserved for movement. These sensors are constantly beaming lasers at the headset to discover its orientation and position in the room, translating that into VR movement. Now the user can make a few steps either way, but how does he or she move down the VR hallway? By using two nunchuck controllers and pressing buttons on them, meaning the best VR experience on the market right now is still just barely above typical console gameplay, but costs at least five times as much. Oh, and a VR headset can't function without a beefy desktop computer that can run the gamut.

Seeing how many young adults live at essentially poverty levels, which includes living in shoebox apartments where they essentially don't have enough room to stretch their feet[66], a VR experience like that is simply unreachable. The closest they'll get to VR is watching someone else do it on YouTube or paying a couple of bucks for a few minutes on a VR roller coaster at a shopping mall. VR technology is too expensive, cumbersome and leisurely to be enjoyed by every person. In comparison, the "Doom" experience was instantly accessible to anyone with a computer who could grab a few minutes of free time, and even multiplayer could be done locally, without internet access.

There's also something about human vision that doesn't gel with wearing VR headgear for an extended period, causing headaches and nausea. VR goggles have a refresh rate just like monitors, so it looks like problems are caused by a mismatch between the refresh rate in our brain optical center and that shown by the goggles, which begs the question – what is the optical center's refresh rate anyway? Now we're essentially trying to hack the brain *without understanding how it works*. Fiddling with these things might cause tremendous long-term harm to a generation weaned on VR, as they won't know anything is wrong until it's already too late to reverse course. So, how do VR headgear manufacturers solve this issue? By simply avoiding it altogether.

Feelreal[67] is a wearable VR headset that promises the ability to *smell* things in video games and videos. The main problem is that it only works with a limited number of supported games, one of which is an open-world fantasy hack&slash Skyrim, and a couple of videos. So, not a lot of content, which is the same problem that buried ambitious

---

[66]https://www.youtube.com/watch?v=Q4FoAr8i26g

[67]https://feelreal.com/

TV sets from much more reputable manufacturers. Apparently, Feelreal works by reading aroma tracks that are embedded in the video data to release wafts of smells from the attachment that hold nine capsules out of 255 available. Feelreal also promises an accurate experience of wind, rain, heat, and vibration at the weight of 7oz or about 200g, with a battery life of four hours.

Feelreal is a typical VR headset that tries to make money off of the craze but doesn't actually *solve any problems*. We've been running around in circles trying to create VR for at least 40 years, and nobody except Carmack brought us any closer to it. What Carmack realized is that our hardware is nowhere near powerful enough to create the equivalent of a holodeck, let alone one whose graphical fidelity provides enjoyment.

Carmack was aiming at a complete immersion in the digital world, like in the movie *The Matrix,* but it seems we should lower the bar considerably and just find whatever works rather than aiming at the lofty goal of graphical perfection. We can never match what fiction writers can produce, so the reasonable option is to focus on producing what works *right now*. There's a reason why Carmack mentioned *Star Trek* as inspiration; all our notions about VR come from popular culture, such as movies, so let's analyze these types of media to see what they got right about VR.

In 1992, we were treated to *The Lawnmower Man*[68], a trippy science fiction horror movie starring Pierce Brosnan, in which a feeble-minded kid gets involved in secret experiments involving virtual reality, turning him into a homicidal genius. In the movie, the poor kid is strapped to a centrifuge and frantically spun around to somehow fuse his mind with the cyberspace, which makes for some cool visuals, but its apparent scriptwriters had no clue how or why VR works. Any attempts at AR or VR will look to *minimize* movement of the body since even the slightest discrepancy between

---

[68]https://www.imdb.com/title/tt0104692/?ref_=fn_al_tt_4

perceived and actual movement will inevitably cause motion sickness and claustrophobia.

1999 brought us *The Matrix*[69], a fantastic trilogy featuring a young hacker, Neo, who discovers the world he's been living in his entire life is completely artificial, and he's actually kept alive in a womb-like pod, where machines drain the body heat of humanity for energy or some such. Despite bringing us the term "taking the red pill", the trilogy is sorely lacking when it comes to explaining how or why VR works. Technical details are once again the Achilles' heel of the story, but a curious detail prominently featuring in the trilogy is that humans are plugged into the Matrix through a jack at the base of the skull. Cool visual detail, but this is highly unlikely ever to work since the risk of infection, or internal injury would be way too high. Actual VR interface would likely be minimally invasive and disposable rather than surgically installed in the body.

This tells you everything you need to know about virtual reality, namely that nobody has a clue how it's meant to work or why. In that regard, we're like those nineteenth-century futurists who imagined the future with ugly robotic servants where plenty of gadgets like autonomous vacuum cleaners are sold precisely because of their neat design rather than any inherent functionality. So, the big lesson is that advancement of IoT, AR, and VR technology will be driven by the free market demands, which will always come down to functional and beautiful design, and gadgets will be minimally intrusive and won't require any legroom.

One thing no futurist could ever imagine is that we'll be richer than any other generation in the history of the world. We're able to afford all the most beautiful gadgets, not because we need their functionality but simply because we enjoy how they look. Instead of clunky robots and bulky contraptions, we have smaller and sleeker

---

[69]https://www.imdb.com/title/tt0133093/?ref_=fn_al_tt_1

technology, and by the looks of it, this trend will continue until we finally arrive at functional and beautiful VR headgear.

Chapter 17 – Our Future

The past is full of shamefully wrong predictions about technology, with a couple of solid ones that turned out way more precise than expected. Let's examine them side by side and see why ones failed and others succeeded. Prophesying is such a thankless task, but it can also be a very exciting window into the future if approached cautiously. With that in mind, let's jump right in.

Minority Report[70] starring Tom Cruise tells the story of a pre-crime unit – basically psychic detectives – who can tap into streams of information coursing through them to discover crime and thus arrest warrants can be issued before the crime happens. These psychics spend their time cooped up in their pods where they're submerged in some apparently nourishing goo and never get to see the real world. Sound familiar? Yep, they're in essence total captives of the digital realm we mentioned earlier, who lost all their ability to function in the real world.

---

[70]https://www.imdb.com/title/tt0181689/?ref_=fn_al_tt_1

The movie is from 2002 but the book it's based on is from 1956, so it's actually surprising how much it got right. At one point, Tom Cruise enters a concourse where an advertisement scans his iris and recognizes him in a fraction of a second, displaying personalized recommendations and even calling him out by his name, which is eerily close to where we're headed. Tom's character also uses an augmented reality display that looks like a transparent computer screen hanging in midair where he shuffles files and folders with exaggerated hand gestures. That one is mostly a miss because there's no way anyone can repeat those gestures for more than a few minutes at a time.

George Orwell's *Nineteen Eight-Four* describes the dystopian world of the future as imagined in 1949, populated by ominous images of Big Brother who's constantly watching and judging from telescreens. Television was just taking hold in the late 1920s when Orwell wrote his book, and it's clear he saw its negative impact on the society with everyone having this blaring, obnoxious box in their living rooms to the point it became a participant in every conversation, except you couldn't argue with it.

What he got wrong is that he imagined them all universally controlled and wall-sized when what we have today is a wealth of content from all imaginable producers on tinier screens than ever and yet with sharper image quality. The lesson here is that all technology we have today will likely become smaller and smaller, with further fragmentation of content creators and a steady increase in video quality. People in the future will likely be producing their own content and assembling their own cameras and other gadgets out of freely available parts.

Arthur Clarke's *2001: A Space Odyssey,* written in 1968, tells the story of an AI leading the human expedition to Jupiter's moon in search of the destination of a mysterious radio signal triggered by an alien monolith found on the Moon going insane. Clarke's idea of the future was that we'd hit a dead-end until we found an outside influence to kickstart our development beyond that, and the solution will inevitably lead us outside the bosom of Mother Earth. As one famous History Channel presenter put it, "Aliens."

Year 2001 came and went without an AI, let alone one piloting a spaceship, or groundbreaking discoveries of extraterrestrial objects. In many ways, that makes the progress we made since then that much more incredible. We did it on our own! That shows the amazing power of global cooperation and information exchange, which is all we need to live the best lives we can imagine. It's likely that ways of gathering and sharing information will expand and deepen, but always with humans at the driver's wheel. True, we do have neural networks, but so far, all they've done is crunch data and spit out the most relevant conclusions.

In summary, let's put on a pair of rose-tinted glasses and daydream for a bit. IoT has shown itself extremely useful in medicine, automating the dreary exams to check for vital signs, cutting down on paperwork and administrative overhead. We'll likely be having more and more IoT technology doing the doctor's work, especially in rural areas in third world countries where the most basic facilities are inaccessible.

Equipped with high-speed internet that can instantly transmit large quantities of data, a doctor in California could be using a medical drone to do remote surgery on tonsils in Bangladesh while observing the video feed from the drone's camera. Past that, a computer algorithm could observe the doctor at work and then do the surgery automatically after training, with neural networks identifying symptoms and delivering a diagnosis.

A fleet of medical bumblebee drones could deliver vaccines or medicine to wherever needed and have surgically implanted sensors to sting people who haven't taken the shot. The only problem would then be legal uncertainty and liability in cases of doctor error or technology failure, something which we should deal with right now, preferably by creating a legal framework for trans-national IoT.

Technology has allowed us to generate more wealth and equality than ever before. If it keeps going this way, we'll be building a world where everyone shares riches and we can all participate by making quality content. Everything will keep getting smaller and smaller up until it becomes miniaturized and we can't even spot it unless someone points it out. Technology will be embedded into everything, including our clothes and bodies, hopefully voluntarily. Whatever it might end up being, that future will be – our future.

Conclusion

While this book did adopt an obvious tongue-in-cheek approach to IoT, there's an undeniable undertone of exhilaration connected to the entire field. Miniaturization has lowered the bar for entry into the consumer device market and enabled anyone with a bit of spare time to create his or her own line of IoT products to be sold at a 1,000% markup. It's likely that none of these products will be remembered in a couple of years, but they still represent a valiant effort to explore and experiment with what seems the perfect mix of hardware and software. We seem like kids who just discovered firecrackers – what *can't they* blow up? Just like kids with firecrackers, it might not end well.

If you decide to try out one of these IoT gadgets, at least now you know what you're buying. Security is nonexistent, even when it comes to major brand IoT devices; forget about privacy because often the manufacturer will be the one spying on you and then recklessly storing your data where any hacker can access it. As always, legislators are lagging at least 30 years behind the market, though with IoT we can't allow such delay before we set up barriers between us and the outside world.

With IoT, we can all do simple things to make ourselves and the rest of the world safer and sounder, but before that, we have to understand the underlying concepts. As you've seen throughout this book, IoT is no boogeyman or rocket science but a simple evolution of mechanical and digital principles to help us enter the twenty-first century in style, helping us spend less time on our chores and trifles, such as vacuuming and googling things. Our robotic servants are meant to help, but we shouldn't fall in love with the sleek design or cool concept but always mercilessly judge them based on their efficiency.

Glossary

AlphaStar – A **neural network** that beat humans in a real-time strategy video game, "Starcraft 2", in January 2019 under dubious circumstances. It was created by the DeepMind team.

Artificial intelligence – A mechanical mind decoupled from a physical body. It may be seen as superior to humans while in fact being vastly inferior.

Attack surface – The joint weakness of a network that directly correlates to its complexity.

Augmented reality – The placement of a digital overlay on top of the physical world. It's normally done using goggles or headgear. It's achievable right now. See **virtual reality**.

Banner blindness – The willful ignorance of banners that should be heeded since the information they contain turned out vague and useless.

Big Data – Self-referential, encyclopedic data on events that reveal the habits of people who participated in them.

Bio-robotics – Using analog beings as living carriers of digital devices.

Bricking – Turning an electronic device into the equivalent of a brick through malware or clumsy modification. It's usually irreversible.

Brute-force attack – Randomly guessing a password. **Hackers** will generally try a list of weakest passwords before giving up and moving on.

Business intelligence – Gathering and utilizing data on an enterprise level.

Closed source – Computer code hidden from the general public but still usable. It's meant to provide **security through obscurity**.

Computer code – Machine equivalent of a genetic code. Unlike actual genes, computer code is unable to mutate or update itself to match the environment. **Machine learning** is meant to provide that capability to machines.

Cybersecurity – Deterring **hackers** using cheaper, simpler and more reliable methods than they use for hacking.

DDoS – Distributed Denial of Service. It uses a multitude of sources to tie a website's resources, so it becomes unresponsive to legitimate users.

Devil's Ivy – Hacking attack on gSOAP, development toolkit for **IoT**.

Dictionary attack – Simple hacking attack during which an attacker tries to log into an account using a list of publicly available username/password combinations.

Feature creep – Expanding the original scope of any software or platform way beyond what it's meant to sustain.

Feelreal – A VR headset attachment that allows the wearer to experience smells assigned to the VR data.

Firmware – Essential code baked into the device.

Gamification – Turning everyday actions into a video game using **augmented reality**.

Hackers – Cyber attackers. They use simple, cheap and straightforward methods to attack remote digital systems constantly.

IoT – The Internet of Things, a haphazard networking of gadgets.

IPv4 – A digital address assignment protocol that's rapidly nearing its end-of-life date.

IPv6 – An upgraded IPv4 protocol. It has a staggering number of addresses, making it fit for IoT.

Limbic system – The core of the brain. Highly predictable by **neural networks**.

Machine learning – Overcoming limitations of static programming in computers by giving them the ability to adapt to the environment. It's meant to produce a "smart" robot that should be able to solve any given problem on its own.

Metadata – Data on data, such as how many miles a car drove, but not where, when or at what speed. It can be used for tracking if aggregated in **Big Data**.

Neural networks – Artificial neurons arranged in consensus data processing structures.

Open source – A software program free for everyone to review, use and edit. Mozilla Firefox is one example.

Predictive analytics – A corporate analysis of **Big Data** to predict behavior trends.

Robots – Thinking, working machines. They are meant to be independent yet obedient.

Security through obscurity – Evading **hackers** by hiding devices and protocols among a huge number of dead-ends.

SOAP – Coding framework used in **IoT** devices.

Virtual reality – Total immersion in the digital world. Theoretically indistinguishable from actual reality, as in the movie, *The Matrix*. It's unknown how to accomplish it.

VPN – A network that can be grafted onto a device to intercept or block traffic.

Wisdom of the crowd – Curious property of crowds to correctly estimate variables when their answers are averaged out.

Check out another book by Neil Wilkins

www.ingramcontent.com/pod-product-compliance
Lightning Source LLC
LaVergne TN
LVHW020054080526
838200LV00083B/177